"It's not often I want to pick up my life and move, but after reading *Tahini Baby* cover to cover, it's safe to say that I would like to be Eden's neighbor. You could open the book, flip to any page, and know that you're looking at a winning recipe. This one is absolutely not to be missed! Twelve outta ten!"

—**Gaby Dalkin,** *New York Times* bestselling author of *What's Gaby Cooking*

"Eden's second cookbook may just be more triumphant than her first! It's packed with the zestiest, most drool-worthy recipes; overflows with warmth; and overdelivers on her playful, signature style. *Tahini Baby* is the baby I didn't know I needed. It will reinvigorate your veggies and inspire you to drizzle, schmear, and sop up every sunshiney drop of kitchen goodness with joy and abandon!"

—**Gail Simmons,** food expert, TV host, and author of *Bringing It Home*

"As my body is nearly 25 percent tahini, I can steadily relate to Eden's *Tahini Baby*. Jokes aside—this is a fresh, fun, and exciting book that will make you feel like you're cooking with Eden and her beautiful family in her stunning home kitchen."

—**Mike Solomonov,** chef and *New York Times* bestselling author of *Zahav*

"I love this book! Eden's magnetic personality and irresistible cooking leap off every page, coaxing you into the kitchen to make her delicious, easy—but never boring—recipes. Guiding us through every step—from creating the ultimate pantry to meals for every occasion and craving—Eden delivers on dishes that are as fun as they are fulfilling."

—**Adeena Sussman,** *New York Times* bestselling author of *Shabbat* and *Sababa*

"I want to cook everything in this book! Eden uses Middle Eastern flavors to create veggie-forward recipes that are exciting, delicious, and—best of all—fun. From gorgeous 'wow salads' to mouthwatering mains, *Tahini Baby* is packed with inspiration for vegetable lovers."

—**Jeanine Donofrio,** *New York Times* bestselling author of *Love & Lemons: Simple Feel Good Food*

"In more ways than one, Eden speaks my culinary language fluently—a meze of bold, vibrant, and herbaceous flavors that are effortlessly plant-forward. *Tahini Baby* echoes just that. Recipes best shared with friends and family, a sprinkle of Aleppo, a squeeze of lemon, and of course, a drizzle of tahini!" —**Athena Calderone,** author of *Cook Beautiful*

TAHINI
BABY

bright, everyday recipes that happen to be vegetarian

TAHINI BABY

eden grinshpan

with rachel holtzman

photography by chris bernabeo

AVERY

an imprint of Penguin Random House

New York

AVERY

an imprint of Penguin Random House LLC
penguinrandomhouse.com

Most Avery books are available at special quantity discounts
for bulk purchase for sales promotions, premiums, fundraising,
and educational needs. Special books or book excerpts
also can be created to fit specific needs. For details, write
SpecialMarkets@penguinrandomhouse.com.

Library of Congress Cataloging-in-Publication Data

Names: Grinshpan, Eden, author. | Holtzman, Rachel, author.
Title: Tahini baby : bright, everyday recipes that happen
    to be vegetarian / Eden Grinshpan; with Rachel Holtzman.
Description: New York: Avery, 2025. | Includes index.
Identifiers: LCCN 2024011303 (print) |
    LCCN 2024011304 (ebook) | ISBN 9780593713426 (hardcover) |
    ISBN 9780593713433 (epub)
Subjects: LCSH: Cooking, Middle Eastern. | Vegetarian cooking—
    Middle East. | LCGFT: Cookbooks.
Classification: LCC TX725.M628 G755 2025 (print) | LCC TX725.
    M628 (ebook) | DDC 641.5/6360956—dc23/eng/20240314
LC record available at https://lccn.loc.gov/2024011303
LC ebook record available at https://lccn.loc.gov/2024011304

Printed in China
10 9 8 7 6 5 4 3 2 1

Book design by Ashley Tucker

For Ido, my best friend and love of my life. Thank you for always holding my hand, believing in me, and helping me accomplish my dreams. I can do anything with you by my side.

And for my girls, Ayv and Romi, this book is for you. The joy I see on your faces when your hands are covered in butter and you're completely dusted with flour while sitting on the counter across from me is probably the best thing I have experienced in my life. The pride is indescribable; there are no words that could truly express my love for you two. You are my world.

CONTENTS

continues ➡

CONTENTS

INTRODUCTION

When I sent my first book, *Eating Out Loud*, into the world, it was with the hope that I could inspire people to get into the kitchen and just *loosen up*. I wanted everyone to see how easy it is to create bold, fresh dishes that don't take themselves too seriously and use only grocery store standbys and a handful of Middle Eastern staples. If they felt like getting a little frisky with new-to-them ingredients like preserved lemons or tahini, or had a dance party while they babysat their chicken soup on the stove, or started putting labaneh on everything, or got all up in their meals with their hands, then I did my job right.

When it came to thinking about what my next book should be about, I didn't need to look much further than the feedback I was getting from my readers and social media followers: yes to big, bold flavors that didn't require more effort than throwing a bunch of shit in a pan™; yes to not having to go to the grocery store for every single recipe because we're reaching for a solid rotation of ingredients and condiments; yes to serving pretty much everything in one big, delicious pile and swabbing it up with good bread; but most of all, yes to putting veggies front and center on the table.

So *Tahini Baby* was a no-brainer: more simple recipes that can be endlessly mixed and matched for meals and leftovers, more fun with new Middle Eastern and Mediterranean ingredients and condiments (and more love for those I already covered in the first book), *especially* tahini. I mean, as if I could ever get enough of that rich, creamy, drizzly perfection. But also I *am* a Tahini Baby; these flavors and culinary traditions are what I was raised on both in my Toronto home and during my summers in Israel. But, more than anything, I wanted to really lean in to the veggie goodness that tahini and its sister sauces help elevate to the next level. In fact, let's make it all veg.

Don't get me wrong, this girl will always love her roast chicken and my husband Ido's signature meatballs. But most of the time, whether I'm cooking for my family or for company, the dishes on my table just so happen to be vegetarian—lowercase v—as in not a label but a delicious approach to cooking, and no one wonders where the meat is. I've been eating veg-forward food for most of my life. From my safta's (grandma's) baba ganoush that she loaded up with the sweetest cherry tomatoes, garlic, and lots of extra-virgin olive oil and served as a light lunch; to grabbing a buttery, flaky Turkish boureka stuffed with the creamiest feta at the shuk in Tel Aviv; to eating falafel after falafel after falafel from the street carts, these dishes perfectly sum up the sunshine-soaked, Mediterranean breeze-tousled, spice-infused, culture-blended vibe that is on offer in the Levant, the expanse of the Middle East that includes modern-day Israel, Jordan, Palestine, Syria, Turkey, Iraq, Egypt, Greece, Cyprus, and Lebanon. It's also proof that vegetables are so much more than side dishes.

Middle Eastern and Mediterranean food has always recognized the power of the plant. To cook these recipes is to perfect the art of taking something really humble and making it unbelievably tasty. Ask anyone who's ever sat down to a bowl of hummus for lunch—that shit is sat-is-fy-ing. You don't sit there and wonder why you didn't get the lamb sprinkled on top. No, you wonder how you've ever had as perfect a meal as a whole bunch of chickpeas blended up with a whole bunch of sesame seeds. For me, that's so much of what Middle Eastern cooking is: a celebration of fresh produce, grains, and legumes, prepared with minimal fuss and layers upon layers of textures and flavors, begging for all the dipping and picking you can handle—without ever feeling like meat is missing (because it's really not).

This book is my way of introducing you to a new way to veg. I want everyone to see that vegetables can hold it down on the table, whether you're throwing together a casual mess of dips and spreads for grazing, having your first meal of the day, putting together lunch from a few made-in-advance components in the fridge, or feeding your family (or just yourself) dinner. Because yes, veggies can be filling mains too—we're talking *substanch*. But most importantly, these dishes are what I like to call "food for real life." They're meant to be quick, multipurpose, versatile, and customizable to suit a wide range of palates (translation: Your kids will eat them!).

Like my first book, *Tahini Baby* is a mix of well-loved Middle Eastern–inspired dishes (with a little refresh) and twists on old-school favorites. There will be recognizable classics like Fast 'n' Fresh Harissa, Herby Olive Oil Challah, and Hawaij "Chicken" Soup. And remixes like Eggplant Schnitzel with Spiced Harissa Tomato Sauce and Garlicky Tahini, Smoky Shakshuka Sandies, and Ultimate Shroom Shawarma. Because I want you to get as comfortable as possible cooking with these flavors, I'll introduce you to all the condiments and spices that I consider must-haves in my fridge and pantry, including new DIY additions such as Labaneh Balls, Preserved Lemon Toum, and Grated Tomato for Everything. There will also be an epic bread chapter—because nothing brings a meal together like fresh-from-the-oven bread slathered in all manner of herbs, spices, and cheeses—with standouts like Jerusalem Bagel Dinner Rolls; Za'atar Laffa; and Challah Khachapuri with Eggs, Herbs, and All the Cheese. And of course, this book wouldn't be complete without an insane lineup of desserts, each of them a love letter to Middle Eastern and Mediterranean ingredients. From Pull-Apart Tahini Rugelach to Sage-Honey Semifreddo, and from Honey-Sesame Candied Matzo to Salty Vanilla Bean Krembo Tart (Ido's childhood in a bite), I've got your sweet treats covered.

But what it all comes down to is that this book is about food that makes you feel good. With their vibrant colors and bright, balanced flavors, these dishes can only be described as *happy-making*. No matter who you're sharing them with (or not), eating well and having a great time doing it is the entire assignment. Not to mention the fact that munching on a whole bunch of veg is a surefire way to put a little pep in your step. Plus, you'll love how much flexibility and creativity these recipes allow for when you're shopping at the market, because nothing is as versatile as a veggie-based recipe. (Swaps and substitutions welcome here! We'll get into it more when we start cooking.)

And if I could put on my mom hat for a moment, I also have to say that making these dishes for my girls is my way of not only sharing food that holds so many memories for me but also instilling a love for and curiosity about all kinds of ingredients. One of my favorite weekend activities is bringing them grocery shopping or to the farmers' market. I let the girls explore the produce and take the lead if there's something they are into. Then, when it's time to put that ingredient to work, they get to see how it's prepared and how it tastes when it's done. Parenting isn't always all dance parties and rainbows, but small moments like these feel like really big wins sometimes. And knowing that I'm passing down traditions while also opening their eyes to the wide world of veggies out there, well, let's just say someone around here must be chopping onions . . .

Quite honestly, these recipes are all five-star must-makes that I couldn't be more excited to share. They're the saucy, hearty, zippy, creamy, crunchy, tasty goodness I'm craving all day, every day. And yeah, they just so happen to be vegetarian. So go ahead and get in there, pick something that speaks to you. Then pick another. And another. Play, make a mess, make mistakes—it doesn't matter because I promise that you'll still end up with something delicious. And as always, I'll be there for you every step of the way!

xo, eden

the tahini baby pantry

When it comes to **keeping my cooking simple**, I don't fuck around. Whether I'm feeding just me, me and Ido, the girls, my extended family, or a houseful of friends, the same rules are always going to apply: The technique, **straightforward**. The flavors, **layered**. And the ingredients, a combination of fresh produce and staple dried goods (pasta, legumes) **all dressed up** with a go-to rotation of Middle Eastern spices. The recipes in this book follow these exact same rules, which is why I wanted to spend a little time walking you through the spices that you'll see called for throughout the book. (Seriously, these are not going to die a quiet death in your spice drawer!) I promise that you'll use them over and over again—a goal of mine when developing recipes; I live to use up every last bit in the jar. My recommendation is to collect them as you need them, then consider keeping them on hand so you'll always have what you need to **whip up something amazing** whenever the mood strikes.

aleppo pepper

This pepper variety originated in Aleppo, Syria, and is now found in cooking traditions across the Middle East. The peppers are semidried, seeded, and crushed, creating nice, plump, slightly oily flakes. Aleppo packs less heat than crushed red chile flakes, but it's fruity and savory in a way that enhances the flavor of whatever you're sprinkling it over (which is pretty much every dish in this book).

baharat

Similar to curry powders, baharat is really just a spice blend (it literally means "spices" in Arabic) that can include any number of ingredients depending on where in the Middle East you are or whose house you're at. And just like curry, it's the kind of spice drawer flavor bomb that you can add to a dish and know that you'll be covered in the delish department.

Note: If you can't find baharat at the store, just mix together ¼ cup toasted ground cumin, 1 tablespoon ground coriander, 1 tablespoon sweet paprika, ½ teaspoon ground cinnamon, ½ teaspoon ground cloves, and ½ teaspoon freshly ground black pepper. Store in an airtight container for up to 1 month.

caraway

Also known as Persian cumin, this pungent, anisey spice was first discovered by the Greeks and is now cultivated all over the world, including in North Africa and the Middle East. It's what I reach for when I want to add instant warmth and a little unique somethin'-somethin' to a dish.

cardamom

Cardamom is one of the most ancient spices, originating in India and Egypt. Now you'll find it both in whole form (pods) or ground in a number of Middle Eastern dishes, especially teas, rice, and desserts. I love it for the warm, sweet, floral, subtly minty flavor it has and keep a stash of pods in my spice drawer, which I can grind as needed (to ensure the best possible flavor)—a great reason to have a mortar and pestle handy.

cinnamon

You're probably very familiar with this one, most likely in sweet preparations. But this woody, earthy, slightly sweet spice is used across the Middle East in savory dishes too.

TAHINI, BABY

I will never forget when I heard chef Mike Solomonov call tahini the Israeli "mother sauce," which is 100 percent accurate and 100 percent how I've viewed it ever since. Tahini is a major player in Middle Eastern cuisine; you find it drizzled over and folded into a huge number of traditional preparations. For good reason: It lends toasty richness and depth of flavor to everything it touches. Plus, tahini is packed with calcium and is a good source of protein (not a small detail when cooking vegetarian meals) plus iron, magnesium, vitamins B and E, healthy fats, and anti-inflammatory and antioxidant properties. I'm not this person, but I'm just going to say it: It's a healthy fucking sauce. And yeah, it makes every single thing it touches more satisfying and delicious. My obsession with tahini runs deep and forever will. I don't just love tahini, baby, I *am* Tahini Baby. I was raised on it, my kids have been raised on it, and now it's your turn to join the fam.

If you're gonna use tahini, you gotta do it right. Look for one that's made from high-quality sesame seeds (the best are from Humera, Ethiopia, and have a sweeter flavor) that have been soaked, hulled (which creates a lighter, less bitter flavor), toasted, then ground in small batches. There are tons of great tahini varieties you can now find in grocery stores and online, but two US brands that stand out to me are Seed + Mill and Soom (which both also happen to be female-owned businesses, win-win). I highly recommend trying several brands for comparison before deciding what your "house" tahini will be. You want to be sure to love the flavor straight from the jar. It shouldn't be too bitter, and it shouldn't be too oily. Whatever you do, don't value shop; this is not the place to skimp, because you can taste a subpar tahini. Plus, tahini will last for months in your fridge. (Although, if I have anything to do with it, that will hopefully not be the case.)

When used in moderation, it lends a deep sultriness to a dish, so don't go thinking that your stew is going to taste like a pumpkin spice latte.

coriander

Here we're actually talking about coriander *seeds*, not to be confused with the leafy plant we know as cilantro in North America but the rest of the world calls coriander. Coriander was one of the most used spices in medieval Arab cuisine, and it's stuck around because there's not a dish that's not more delicious thanks to its earthy, tart, floral flavor. I use both whole coriander seeds and ground coriander in my cooking; each has a time and a place.

cumin

This is easily one of the most popular spices in Middle Eastern cooking and is what gives things like falafel and shawarma that rich, warm, earthy flavor. You can use it ground or as whole seeds, which, when toasted and sprinkled over a dish or stirred into a dressing, lend instant depth and texture.

dried black limes

Also known as Persian limes or loomi, these sun-dried limes got their start in Persian Gulf countries like Oman, Iraq, and Iran but have now made their way through a wider swath of Middle Eastern cooking traditions. You'll see them used whole, sliced, or ground (I like using a Microplane to freshly grate what I need). They add a distinct sour lift to a dish, as though they're passing on all that sunshine they soaked up.

fenugreek leaves and seeds

The fenugreek plant is native to the Mediterranean, but you see the seeds and leaves popping up in dishes from Middle Eastern neighbors like Iran, Yemen, and Morocco. Whether you're infusing these into braises, sauces, or teas or stirring them into stews, both the leaves and the seeds impart such a unique fragrance. The seeds have a curry-like flavor and smell, while the leaves have an unbelievable maple syrup–like essence.

orange blossom and rose water

Both of these pantry staples have deep ties to Arab culture across the Middle East. You'll see these distilled essences used in dishes (especially desserts) or iconic self-care.

(Orange blossom or rose water bath or facial spritz? Yes and yes.) Just be forewarned, these flavors can be very potent, so in order to keep our dishes from tasting like bathwater, we're going to use a very light hand. If we've done our job well—and these recipes will not lead you astray—you'll have a dish with an alluring suggestion of orange or rose.

paprika

This is a spice drawer must and a Middle Eastern cooking staple. It's made from dried and ground peppers, either bell peppers, chile peppers, or a mixture of both, which is why it ranges from mild to hot to smoky. But no matter which type you use, paprika lends body and richness to a dish, not to mention a gorgeous ruby-red color.

pomegranate molasses

This tart, syrupy condiment is almost like the aged balsamic vinegar of Middle Eastern cooking. It's perfect for finishing dishes, as well as making sauces and vinaigrettes, because its sweet-sour pop of flavor brings all the other ingredients to life.

Note: If you can't find it, you can make your own: In a medium pot, combine 6 cups of pomegranate juice with ¾ cup of sugar and the juice of 1 lemon. Bring to a boil over medium-high heat, reduce to a simmer, and cook until you have a nice, thick syrup. Store in a jar with a fitted lid in the fridge for up to 1 month.

savory hawaij

This is another one of those spice blends that can vary depending on where you are and who you're talking to, but the classic combination for this Yemeni cooking staple includes black pepper, cumin, cardamom, and turmeric. From soups and stews, to rice and vegetable dishes, to barbecue-style rubs, it's a hardworking, versatile blend that never overpowers, just makes everything taste better.

You can find hawaij at Middle Eastern markets or online; just be sure you're buying a savory version and not the sweeter variation that's used for coffee. You could also make your own:

MAKES ½ CUP

2 tablespoons cardamom pods

1½ tablespoons coriander seeds

1 tablespoon cumin seeds

2 teaspoons fenugreek seeds

1 teaspoon whole cloves

2 teaspoons whole black peppercorns

1½ tablespoons ground turmeric

1. In a medium skillet, combine the cardamom, coriander, cumin, fenugreek, cloves, and peppercorns. Toast over medium heat until the spices are fragrant, about 2 minutes.

2. Remove the cardamom seeds from the pods and discard the shells.

3. In a high-speed blender, combine the toasted spices with the turmeric and blend until evenly ground. Store the mixture in a sealed container in a cool, dry place for up to 1 year.

sumac

Keep this between you and me, but sumac is my favorite spice. It packs a bright and citrusy yet earthy punch that makes dishes taste like the best versions of themselves, which is why it makes the perfect finishing sprinkle to add that little extra pop. I also love the fact that it's made from a berry that grows wild on every continent except South America and Antarctica.

turmeric

You know and love her as the spice world's anti-inflammatory, antioxidant golden girl, but I'm a big fan because turmeric's deep, rich earthiness grounds a dish. The fact that it makes everything it touches a sunshiny yellow (including your clothes and nails—proceed with caution, especially after a manicure) is a major bonus.

za'atar

To me, the fragrance of za'atar is like Tel Aviv markets in a jar. It's a signature combination of wild oregano, sumac, sesame seeds, and salt, giving whatever it's sprinkled into a savory, appetite-stoking allure. The pro move is to mix it with olive oil and drizzle it over fresh-baked bread and roasted veg.

Note: If you can't find za'atar at the store, just blend ½ cup dried oregano until it is a fine powder and combine it with a heaping ¼ cup sumac, ⅓ cup toasted sesame seeds, and ½ teaspoon kosher salt. Store in an airtight container for several months.

condiments, dips, and all the noshes

If I told you that I had the ultimate hack for making an unending variety of absurdly quick, intensely delicious, and never-boring meals, wouldn't you want to know it? Great! Because this chapter has it. Condiments, dips, and salatim, or little nosh-y salads, are the key to not only preserving your sanity in the kitchen but also **amping up pretty much any dish**. These recipes are going to bring even more layers of brightness, zippiness, richness, and heat to your cooking (aka make you actually want to eat your veggies), and they're basically all designed to be stashed in your fridge, mixed and matched, swapped and subbed, so you can use them throughout the week on pretty much any dish as a **drizzle**, **dip**, or side. And to sweeten the deal, I've not only curated the best of the best here (we're talking best-of hummus, baba, tahini sauce, zhoug, etc.), but I've also figured out *the easiest and quickest ways possible* to make each of these recipes so you always **look like a rock star** in the kitchen, even when you're just tossing a bunch of things in a blender. If you dive in and pick a few favorites, a solid meal (or snack or app) is truly only minutes away.

With each recipe, I've listed specific dishes in this book that call for it as a condiment so you can get some inspiration and see how to put these spreads to work. But know that they are all **the perfect addition** to just about any savory recipe here, so they are majorly worth your time and space in your fridge to have handy for last-minute dressing and drizzling.

celery zhoug

1 teaspoon coriander seeds

½ teaspoon cumin seeds

2 cardamom pods, crushed and seeds reserved, or ½ teaspoon ground cardamom

2 medium celery stalks, roughly chopped

½ bunch fresh cilantro, stems and leaves (about 1 packed cup)

½ bunch fresh flat-leaf parsley, stems and leaves (about 1 packed cup)

½ cup refined avocado or grapeseed oil

2 to 3 medium serrano chiles (depending on how much heat you like), stemmed

Juice of ½ lemon

1 medium garlic clove, peeled

¾ teaspoon kosher salt

Note: The zhoug will separate when it sits in the fridge, but you just have to give it a good mix to bring it back to its original just-made state.

Zhoug is a Yemeni hot sauce. At its core, it's fresh on fresh on fresh with tons of herbs, coriander, and cumin, plus a punch of green heat, but it's common to see different interpretations and variations. A few years ago I had one made with celery, and my mind was blown by how its sweet, floral notes and refreshing crunchiness lightened everything up even more. Now it has essentially become our house hot sauce, and we spread it on anything and everything.

1. In a small skillet, combine the coriander, cumin, and cardamom. Toast over medium-low heat until aromatic, 2 to 3 minutes. Remove the pan from the heat.

2. Add the spices to a high-speed blender with the celery, cilantro, parsley, oil, chiles, lemon juice, garlic, and salt and blend until smooth. (Some of the spices might stay chunky, and that's okay.)

3. Store in a sealed container in the fridge for up to 1 week (see Note).

SCHMEAR IT ON...

Tahini Party Plate (page 85)

Cheddar Scallion Matzo Brei with Zhoug and Za'atar (page 97)

Lebanese Breakfast Sandy (page 101)

Crispy, Crunchy Potato Chunks with Preserved Lemon Toum and Golden Amba Pepper Sauce (page 156)

Crispy Artichokes with Crème Fraîche and Zhoug (page 164)

Ultimate Shroom Shawarma (page 180)

Arayes: Lebanese Stuffed Pitas with Cauliflower, Mushrooms, and Walnuts (page 193)

Green Olive and Zhoug Cheesy Toast (page 213)

Challah Khachapuri with Eggs, Herbs, and All the Cheese (page 225)

Turkish Boureka Three Ways (page 218)

fast 'n' fresh harissa

1½ tablespoons Aleppo pepper or red chile flakes

1 tablespoon coriander seeds, toasted until fragrant in a dry pan

1 teaspoon cumin seeds, toasted until fragrant in a dry pan

2 teaspoons paprika

½ teaspoon smoked paprika

½ teaspoon caraway seeds

1 medium red bell pepper, halved and seeded

½ cup refined avocado or grapeseed oil

Heaping ¼ cup tomato paste

2 red long-hot chiles, stemmed

3 medium garlic cloves, peeled

Juice of ½ lemon

1 teaspoon kosher salt

This North African spice blend paste is like hot sauce's smoky, sultry, more interesting pen pal from abroad. For years I would make my own by rehydrating dried chiles and blitzing them up, which is worth it for many reasons, but saving time is not one of them. By using fresh chiles as a base, you can develop that same savory richness in half the time, so you never have an excuse to not have a jar handy.

1. In a high-speed blender, combine the Aleppo, coriander, cumin, paprika, smoked paprika, and caraway. Blend until they're all ground to a powder. Alternatively, you could do this in a spice grinder or with a mortar and pestle.

2. Add the bell pepper, oil, tomato paste, chiles, garlic, lemon juice, and salt and blend until smooth.

3. Store in a sealed container in the refrigerator for up to 1 week.

VARIATION:
harissa mayo

Stir together 2 tablespoons of harissa with 2 tablespoons of mayonnaise and spread on all your sandwiches.

SCHMEAR IT ON...

Tomatoey Green Beans (page 57)

Terracotta Tahini (page 60)

Sticky Jammy Eggplant (page 69)

Crispy, Crunchy Potato Chunks with Preserved Lemon Toum and Golden Amba Pepper Sauce (page 156)

Harissa Honey Carrots with Carrot Top Gremolata and Labaneh (page 167)

Summertime (or Anytime) Stewed Veggie Couscous (page 175)

Eggplant Schnitzel with Spiced Harissa Tomato Sauce and Garlicky Tahini (page 179)

Ultimate Shroom Shawarma (page 180)

Harissa-Roasted Cauliflower and Broccoli with Golden Raisin Gremolata and Toum (page 197)

Tunisian Chickpea Sandwich with All the Fixings (page 214)

Smoky Shakshuka Sandies (page 217)

Harira (page 256)

Egg-Fried Bulgur (page 260)

Spiced Harissa Orecchiette with Garlicky Tahini (page 270)

golden amba pepper sauce

Makes about 1½ cups

1 medium yellow bell pepper, seeded and roughly chopped (see Notes)

⅓ cup refined avocado or grapeseed oil

1 to 2 fresh cayenne chiles (depending on how much heat you like), stemmed

Juice of ½ lemon

2 teaspoons amba powder or store-bought amba sauce (see Notes)

1½ teaspoons kosher salt

1 medium garlic clove, peeled

½ teaspoon ground turmeric

Notes: You can use a red or orange bell pepper if that's all you have—the sauce just won't be the same bright yellow.

Amba powder may also be labeled as dried mango powder. If you can't find it, amchur powder is a good substitute.

Iraq was once home to one of the largest and oldest populations of Jews in the world. And when many of them picked up and left for Israel in the 1950s, they brought this sunshine-in-a-jar sauce with them. Made from unripe mango (or green mango), lemon juice or vinegar, turmeric, and fenugreek, amba has a unique flavor—tangy and tart yet bold with a kick of fresh-pepper heat. It brings depth and personality to anything you drizzle it on, and in my opinion, nothing grilled or wrapped up in a pita or laffa would be complete without it. You can use amba as is (it's one of my favorite condiments), but I like blending it with the peppers and chiles to add some heat and also mellow the amba flavor a bit, which also means you can slather even more of it on.

1. In a high-speed blender, combine the bell pepper, oil, chiles, lemon juice, amba, salt, garlic, and turmeric. Blend until smooth.

2. Store in a sealed container in the fridge for up to 1 week.

SCHMEAR IT on...

Crispy, Crunchy Potato Chunks with Preserved Lemon Toum and Golden Amba Pepper Sauce (page 156)

Ultimate Shroom Shawarma (page 180)

I GOT YOU, BUBBELEH

While we can obviously all agree that making something yourself is going to be super flavorful and special and look nice in your fridge in a pretty little jar, sometimes . . . life. As quick and easy as I've tried to make things—and I really have given you some pretty epic shortcuts for things like DIY harissa paste and preserved lemons—there's not always going to be time, and that's okay. So this is your official permission to grab a jar of amba from Trader Joe's (it's pretty great), a tub of labaneh or toum, or a jar of pre-made baharat. And one day, your season of making your own will be here again.

israeli pickles

6 to 10 small Persian or mini cucumbers (however many fit in your jar), cleaned well

Ice water

8 medium garlic cloves, gently crushed

1 hot pepper of choice, halved lengthwise (optional)

1 tablespoon coriander seeds

1 teaspoon fennel seeds

1 dried bay leaf

1 bunch fresh dill (optional)

2½ tablespoons kosher salt

1¾ to 2 cups filtered water

My love for Israeli pickles runs deep. The briny, garlic-heaven flavor that permeates these pickles (plus their satisfying snap) is simply unmatched, and the likelihood that I could devour the entire jar is high. In fact, I think of them less as a pickle you'd eat alongside a sandwich or burger and more like a little meal all on their own—the drive-by snack of choice in our house. (The girls will devour an entire jar in one sitting.) Finding small Persian or mini cucumbers is key, though; the smaller the cukes, the more intense the flavor will be. And if you're as obsessed with these as I am, feel free to scale up the recipe.

1. Place the cucumbers in a large bowl and cover with ice water. Allow them to soak for 5 to 10 minutes. (This helps keep the cucumbers nice and crisp.)

2. Meanwhile, bring a large pot of water to a boil over high heat. Add a 32-ounce glass jar and its lid and boil for 10 minutes to sterilize them. Use tongs to carefully remove the jar and allow it to steam dry.

3. Drain the cucumbers and place them in the jar with the garlic, hot pepper (if using), coriander, fennel, and bay leaf. Stuff a nice handful of dill into the crevices (if using) and add

the salt. Add enough filtered water to completely submerge the cucumbers, usually about 2 cups.

4. Seal the jar and flip upside down to help mix in the spices and salt. Place the jar in a cool, dark place (I like the inside of my pantry) for 3 days. You may want to place a plate underneath in case any water leaks.

5. Transfer the jar to the fridge. You can start eating the pickles after 3 days in the fridge, but truth be told, they get really good a week or two later. They'll keep for up to 1 month.

condiments, dips, and all the noshes

grated tomato for everything

4 medium tomatoes on the vine

1 medium garlic clove, peeled

1 medium serrano chile, jalapeño, or green long-hot chile, finely chopped (optional)

2 tablespoons extra-virgin olive oil

½ teaspoon kosher salt

The first time I had this Yemeni tomato salsa (called zahawig) was with one of my favorite Yemeni dishes, jachnun (a folded pastry that's traditionally served Shabbat morning and is a must-order if you see it on a menu), and I was completely blown away by how something so simple (literally just tomatoes grated into a bowl with a kiss of garlic and salt) could bring such brightness and acidity to a dish. I later learned that my mother-in-law never serves anything without a chile-fied version of this on the table, and she's right that it works with just about anything you can imagine. I guarantee that if you spoon this over a dish—a bowl of matzo brei, fresh labaneh, a piping-hot boureka—you'll be shocked by how much more than the sum of its parts it is.

1. On the largest holes of a box grater, grate the tomatoes into a medium bowl. Use the smaller holes to grate the garlic and add the chile (if using), olive oil, and salt. Toss to combine.

2. Store in a sealed container in the fridge for up to 2 days, but it really is best served fresh (hence the smaller yield).

SCHMEAR IT ON...

Sumac, Aleppo, and Za'atar Labaneh Balls (page 42)

Tahini Party Plate (page 85)

Cheddar Scallion Matzo Brei with Zhoug and Za'atar (page 97)

Labaneh Feta Boureka (page 220)

Masala Potato Boureka (page 221)

Eggplant and Feta Boureka (page 223)

preserved lemon toum

Makes 1 cup

6 large garlic cloves, peeled

2 tablespoons rinsed and chopped rind of Preserved Lemons (page 67)

1 cup refined avocado or grapeseed oil

⅓ cup fresh lemon juice (about 2 juicy lemons)

1 to 2 egg whites (see Note)

1 teaspoon kosher salt

Note: The egg white is here to help the toum thicken up to a mayo-like consistency. If that doesn't happen for you after using one, I give you permission to add another.

Move over, mayo and aioli, this Lebanese garlic sauce is here to bring the fire . . . literally. It will forever change your mind about how much garlic a dish really needs (hint: it's more), and how much you care whether your significant other can smell your breath from two rooms away (hint: it's less). And because subtlety has never been my strong suit, I also threw in some preserved lemon, resulting in legit flavor-bomb status. Use this on any savory dish where you'd add a dollop of mayo, yogurt, or dressing; top with extra preserved lemon for more pop and brightness, if desired.

1. In a high-speed blender or food processor, combine the garlic and preserved lemon. Add a splash of the oil and blend just to break everything up. With the blender running on medium speed, add a bit more oil, followed by a splash of the lemon juice. Continue alternating the two, which will help the toum emulsify.

2. Once all the oil and lemon juice have been combined, add 1 egg white and the salt. Blend on high speed until the toum thickens to a mayo-like consistency, about 2 minutes. If after that point the mixture has not thickened, add the second egg white.

3. Store in a sealed container in the fridge for up to 5 days.

SCHMEAR IT ON . . .

Crispy, Crunchy Potato Chunks with Preserved Lemon Toum and Golden Amba Pepper Sauce (page 156)

Squash and Walnut Kibbeh with Tahini, Sumac, and Lemon (page 191)

Harissa-Roasted Cauliflower and Broccoli with Golden Raisin Gremolata and Toum (page 197)

Tunisian Chickpea Sandwich with All the Fixings (page 214)

sumac, aleppo, and za'atar labaneh balls

Makes 20 to 22 balls (or about 3 cups)

2 (500-gram) containers full-fat Greek yogurt

Juice of ½ lemon

2 teaspoons kosher salt

Sumac, Za'atar (page 25), and/or Aleppo pepper, for serving (optional)

Extra-virgin olive oil, as needed

Notes: I like storing these in Weck canning jars because the wide-mouth shape makes it easier to scoop out the balls. And don't throw away the oil when you're done— you can still cook with it; I love using it to roast veggies.

If keeping these at room temperature doesn't sit well with you, store them in the fridge; just make sure to let them sit at room temperature for a couple hours before using them to let the olive oil return to its liquid state.

You could also make this recipe but skip rolling the labaneh into balls and submerging it in oil. Use it any time labaneh is called for in this book. It will keep in the fridge in a sealed container for up to 2 weeks.

Labaneh is lusciously creamy yogurt and a key player in piling a bunch of tasty things on a plate. I reach for labaneh when I want to balance out all the roasty, toasty flavors that I love, and you can take it a step further by rolling these ready-to-spread balls in Aleppo pepper, sumac, and/or za'atar. Fully submerged in olive oil, they'll last on your counter for months, which means you'll always have a little something to dip or zhuzh—and look like a total balaboosta.

1. Line a tall bowl that will fit in your fridge with cheesecloth.

2. In a second medium bowl, stir together the yogurt, lemon juice, and salt until well combined. Transfer the mixture to the cheesecloth-lined bowl. Wrap up the sides of the cheesecloth to cover the yogurt and tie them over the handle of a wooden spoon or spatula so the loosely tied-up pouch is hanging and not touching the bottom of the bowl. Alternatively, you could tie the cheesecloth tightly around the labaneh and place it in a fine-mesh sieve set on top of a bowl.

3. Place the bowl in the fridge to drain for 48 hours, until the yogurt is thick and easy to roll into neat balls. It's important

that the labaneh rolls together and holds its shape before you place it in the jar and add oil.

4. Bring a large pot of water to a boil over high heat. Add one 19-ounce glass jar (or two 9-ounce jars) and the lid(s) and boil for 10 minutes (see Notes). Use tongs to carefully remove the jar and the lid and allow them to steam dry.

5. Roll the yogurt into golf-ball-size balls. If you like, you can also roll them in the sumac, za'atar, and/or Aleppo to coat. Gently stack the balls in the sterilized jar. Add enough olive oil to cover, then seal and store at room temperature (or in the fridge, if that's your comfort zone; see Notes) for up to 3 months.

baba

safta's baba

Baba ganoush was my dad's mom's all-time most famous dish, which is saying a lot because the woman could cook. With just this preparation, my grandmother, or *safta*, as we say in Hebrew, taught me everything I needed to know about what makes for a great meal: a bowl of creamy, smoky, whipped charred eggplant finished with plenty of fresh cherry tomatoes; garlic; and a slick of olive oil, served simply with good, fluffy bread. With this dish she also taught me what it means to sacrifice in the name of love, since she'd insist on picking out every seed from the eggplant so her boys could have the creamiest possible baba (though, luckily, the eggplants we now get have far fewer seeds). But her legacy lives on because my dad would make this for us, and I now make it for my own kids. You don't need anything more than that to be completely satisfied and happy, but you could also serve this alongside other dips and salads for a salatim-style spread, or even put it out as a condiment alongside your main.

MAKES ABOUT 2 CUPS

3 large eggplants

1 medium garlic clove, peeled

1 teaspoon kosher salt

1 cup halved cherry tomatoes

Extra-virgin olive oil, for serving

Flaky sea salt, for serving

Fresh Challah (page 228) or other fluffy bread, for serving (optional)

1. Preheat a grill or grill pan to high heat.

2. With the tip of your knife, score each eggplant in two places. It doesn't need to be perfect or in the same place every time; this is just so the

recipes continue

condiments, dips, and all the noshes

eggplant doesn't explode on you (it's happened to me, and it's not pretty).

3. Add the eggplants to the grill or grill pan and let the heat do its thing, making sure to keep turning each eggplant so it chars all over. You want it to get black and maybe even white in some places, about 30 minutes total.

4. Transfer the cooked eggplants to a colander in the sink and let the juices run. (The juices can make the dish bitter.) Once they're cool enough to handle, remove all the eggplant skin and stems and discard.

5. Place the eggplant flesh in a medium bowl, then use a Microplane to grate in the garlic. Sprinkle with the salt, then whisk the mixture to give the eggplant a good mash and break up the fibers.

6. Spread the baba ganoush over a plate and serve with the cherry tomatoes on the side or arranged nicely around the edge (just like my safta did it). Give everything a good drizzle of olive oil and give the tomatoes a juicy pinch of flaky salt. Eat as is or with fresh challah (or any fresh bread, if you like).

7. Store the leftovers in a sealed container in the fridge for up to 5 days.

tangy, creamy baba

Baba ganoush doesn't really *need* help in the creamy department, but adding mayo, tahini, or yogurt gives it some extra body and zip.

MAKES ABOUT 2 CUPS

1 recipe Safta's Baba

2 tablespoons full-fat Greek yogurt, tahini, or mayonnaise, plus more to taste

Juice of ½ lemon, if using yogurt or tahini

Extra-virgin olive oil, for serving (optional)

Paprika, for serving (optional)

Fresh Challah (page 228) or other fluffy bread, for serving (optional)

1. After adding the garlic and salt to the charred eggplant, stir in the yogurt, tahini, or mayo. If using yogurt or tahini, also add a squeeze of lemon juice. Whisk to give the eggplant a good mash and break up the fibers. Add more yogurt, tahini, or mayo to taste (up to 2 tablespoons more).

2. Spread the baba ganoush over a plate and finish with either olive oil or a pinch of paprika. Eat as is or with fresh challah (or any fresh bread, if you like).

3. Store leftovers in a sealed container in the fridge for up to 5 days.

SCHMEAR IT ON . . .

Herby Olive Oil Challah (page 228)

Jerusalem Bagel Dinner Rolls (page 232)

Laffa Two Ways (page 236)

Honestly, serve it with anything in this book. It goes with everything.

light-as-air hummus

2 (15-ounce) cans chickpeas, drained and rinsed

1 teaspoon baking soda (see Note)

1 cup tahini

Juice of 1 large lemon (about ¼ cup), plus more for serving

2 medium garlic cloves, peeled

1½ teaspoons kosher salt, plus more to taste

1 teaspoon ground cumin

¾ cup ice water

Extra-virgin olive oil, for serving (optional)

Paprika, for serving (optional)

Garlicky Tahini (page 59), for serving (optional)

Note: In a pinch, I give you full permission to skip the boiling step and go straight to blending.

As I've mentioned before, I am a working mother, which should tell you pretty much everything you need to know about how much spare time I have (zero). I'm also a cook who loves making delicious food. So if I can use a shortcut in my cooking and still arrive at the same tasty result, I'm there. This recipe is a prime example because I will never ever settle for anything less than perfect, silky-smooth hummus. Enter canned chickpeas, which, honest to God, are a gift (which is why I'm still talking about them in yet another cookbook). To give them that optimal extra-creamy, velvety texture, I simmer them with baking soda to tenderize them and help remove the skins. And yet it takes a fraction of the time it would take to cook your chickpeas from scratch, which I just don't think should get in the way of making our hummus dreams come true—and having the ideal base for all the veg.

1. In a large pot, combine the chickpeas and baking soda with 6 cups of water. Bring to a boil over medium-high heat, then reduce the heat to low and let simmer until the chickpeas start breaking down, 15 to 20 minutes. Drain the chickpeas and give them a good shake in the strainer to help remove some of the skins. I don't get too picky about this part, but since the skins will clump together, I do recommend fishing out what you can because your hummus will be all the creamier for it.

2. In a blender, combine the chickpeas with the tahini, lemon juice, garlic, salt, and cumin. Add the ice water along with a few ice cubes (they will make your hummus even creamier) and blend on medium-high speed until the mixture is very smooth, occasionally pausing to scrape down the sides with a spatula, 3 to 5 minutes. Season with more salt, as needed.

3. If desired, serve topped with a drizzle of olive oil and a pinch of paprika; with a pool of garlicky tahini in the center finished with a squeeze of lemon, olive oil, and paprika; or with any of the toppings on page 53.

4. Store in a sealed container in the fridge for up to 1 week.

SCHMEAR IT ON...

Herby Olive Oil Challah (page 228)

Jerusalem Bagel Dinner Rolls (page 232)

Laffa Two Ways (page 236)

hummus . . . with a bunch of different stuff on it

In addition to gifting you the recipe for the gold standard of hummus (page 50), I'm also giving you three options for piling up stuff on top: fresh chopped salad with tahini, baharat-spiced mushrooms with preserved lemons, and tomatoey green beans. Because it doesn't get simpler or more satisfying than a starter/dip/side/complete meal consisting of hummus with stuff on it.

with chopped salad, tahini, lemon, and sumac (aka the perfect lunch)

This is what I make whenever I want to put a smile on Ido's face, and it pretty much sums up my approach to cooking—it's light, it's bright, it's crunchy, it's saucy, and it's perfect for nibbling and grazing. It would make the perfect lunch or dinner on its own or loaded up with things like a jammy egg, jammy eggplant (page 69), and/or Israeli Pickles (page 37). Serve with plenty of fresh laffa (page 236), challah (page 228), or pita.

SERVES 2

3 small Persian or mini cucumbers, finely chopped

2 medium tomatoes on the vine, finely chopped

½ small red onion, finely chopped

6 small radishes, finely chopped

3 tablespoons extra-virgin olive oil, plus more for serving

Juice of ½ lemon

¾ teaspoon kosher salt, plus more to taste

3 cups Light-as-Air Hummus (page 50)

½ cup Garlicky Tahini (page 59)

Large pinch of sumac, for serving

recipes continue

1. In a medium bowl, toss together the cucumbers, tomatoes, onion, and radishes. Add the olive oil, lemon juice, and salt and toss to coat well. Season with more salt, if needed.

2. Divide the hummus between two serving plates and make a well in the center. Fill the inside of each with half of the tahini and top with half of the chopped salad. Finish with a little olive oil and a juicy pinch of sumac.

with baharat mushrooms and preserved lemon relish

Mushrooms are such a great way of adding meaty texture to a dish, and here we're caramelizing them in deeply savory baharat, piling them high on hummus, and finishing things off with a bright pop of preserved lemon relish. To scoop is to fall in love.

SERVES 2

FOR THE PRESERVED LEMON RELISH

4 tablespoons rinsed and finely chopped rind of Preserved Lemons (page 67)

3 tablespoons finely chopped fresh cilantro leaves and stems, plus more whole leaves for garnish

5 tablespoons extra-virgin olive oil

1 medium jalapeño or serrano chile, finely chopped (optional)

Juice of 1 lemon

½ teaspoon kosher salt

FOR THE BAHARAT MUSHROOMS

8 ounces oyster mushrooms, torn into bite-size pieces

4 tablespoons extra-virgin olive oil

2 medium garlic cloves, grated or minced

1½ teaspoons Baharat (page 20)

½ teaspoon kosher salt

FOR ASSEMBLY

3 cups Light-as-Air Hummus (page 50)

recipes continue

1. **Make the relish:** In a medium bowl, combine the preserved lemon rind and cilantro. Add the olive oil, chile (if using), lemon juice, and salt and toss to combine. Set aside.

2. **Make the mushrooms:** In a medium bowl, combine the mushrooms, 2 tablespoons of the olive oil, the garlic, baharat, and salt and mix well.

3. Heat the remaining 2 tablespoons olive oil in a large skillet over medium heat. When the oil shimmers, add the mushrooms, making sure not to crowd the pan or they won't get nice and brown. (You may need to sear them in batches.) Allow the mushrooms to sear, with minimal stirring, until they are crisp and golden on all sides, about 7 minutes. Remove the pan from the heat.

4. **Assemble:** Divide the hummus between two serving plates. Top each with half of the mushrooms and the relish. Finish with cilantro leaves and serve.

with tomatoey green beans

I have really fond memories of eating tangy, tomatoey braised green beans growing up, inspired by a Lebanese dish called loubieh. I wanted to include a recipe for a version that really packs in the smokiness and spice, and I love the idea of spooning these beans warm over hummus because the natural acidity of the tomatoes cuts the earthy richness of the tahini and chickpeas. (Although, they're perfection on their own too.) For how easy it is to toss this all together, it adds up to something pretty magical.

Note: If you like heat, add the harissa. Or you could sub in a fresh red chile or Aleppo pepper.

SERVES 2

¼ cup extra-virgin olive oil, plus more for serving

1 medium yellow onion, finely chopped

1 teaspoon kosher salt, plus more to taste

Freshly ground black pepper to taste

recipe and ingredients continue

condiments, dips, and all the noshes

3 medium garlic cloves, thinly sliced

2 tablespoons tomato paste

2 tablespoons Fast 'n' Fresh Harissa (page 33; optional, see Note, page 57)

1 teaspoon paprika

¼ teaspoon smoked paprika

2 cups chopped tomatoes (about 2 medium tomatoes on the vine) or canned San Marzano tomatoes

1 pound green beans

3 cups Light-as-Air Hummus (page 50)

1. Heat the olive oil in a medium pot over medium-low heat. When the oil shimmers, add the onion and season with the salt and pepper. Sauté, stirring occasionally, until the onion is beginning to turn golden brown, 10 to 15 minutes. Add the garlic and cook for just a couple seconds before stirring in the tomato paste, harissa (if using), paprika, and smoked paprika. Cook just to marry the flavors, about 2 minutes.

2. Stir in the tomatoes and ½ cup of water. Cover the pot and allow the tomatoes to cook down slightly, about 5 minutes. Add the beans and toss to coat. Cover once again and cook until the beans are tender, about 20 minutes. Remove the lid and simmer for another 5 to 10 minutes, until the sauce is just thick enough to cling to the beans. Taste for seasonings and add more if needed to your liking.

3. Divide the hummus between two shallow serving bowls or plates and top each with half of the saucy beans. Finish with a drizzle of olive oil.

garlicky tahini

the condiment to end all condiments

Makes about 3 cups

1½ cups tahini

3 tablespoons fresh lemon juice (about 1 large lemon)

1 teaspoon kosher salt

1 garlic clove, grated

1¼ cups ice water

Notes: Because this makes a big batch, I've also included two variations—herbed and chile'd, and harissa'd—so you can change up the flavor profile if that's what you're in the mood for. Use either of these variations the exact same way you would the original.

Also, you don't necessarily need a blender to make the garlicky or terracotta tahini. I like using it because it gives the sauces lighter body and velvety texture, but you could definitely just throw everything into a bowl and mix with a spoon or whisk.

Did we talk about garlicky tahini in my last book? Yes. Do we need to do it again here? One hundred percent. That's because it's not just a condiment, it's a way of life. There is not a cooking fuck-up or shitty day that tahini, an impossibly creamy and nutty toasted sesame seed paste, cannot fix—especially when it is blended into velvety, garlicky, drizzly perfection. Its savory richness blunts bitter edges (which is particularly key if you're not naturally a vegetable lover), adds body, lends decadence, and just generally makes you wonder whether you should take a bath in whatever it is you're eating. Make a jar. Keep it all week. Use it on *everything*.

1. In a high-speed blender, combine the tahini, lemon juice, salt, and garlic. Add 1 cup of the ice water and blend until smooth. To loosen the sauce, add more ice water as desired.

2. Store in a sealed container in the fridge for up to 1 week.

condiments, dips, and all the noshes

spicy green tahini

MAKES 1 CUP

1 cup Garlicky Tahini

¼ cup packed fresh cilantro leaves

¼ cup packed fresh flat-leaf parsley leaves

¼ cup packed fresh chives

1 medium jalapeño, stemmed (optional if you're not looking for that kick of heat)

Juice of ½ lemon

Kosher salt to taste

1. In a high-speed blender, combine the garlicky tahini with the cilantro, parsley, chives, and jalapeño (if using). Blend until smooth. Season with the lemon juice and salt to wake up the flavors, as needed.

2. Store in a sealed container in the fridge for up to 1 week.

terracotta tahini

MAKES 1¼ CUPS

1 cup Garlicky Tahini

½ cup Fast 'n' Fresh Harissa (page 33)

Fresh lemon juice to taste

Kosher salt to taste

1. In a high-speed blender, combine the garlicky tahini with the harissa and blend until smooth. Season with a little lemon juice and salt to wake up the flavors, as needed.

2. Store in a sealed container in the fridge for up to 1 week.

SCHMEAR IT ON . . .

Tangy, Creamy Baba (page 49)

Hummus . . . with a Bunch of Different Stuff on It (page 53)

Lemon-Braised Leek and Chickpea Masabacha (page 64)

Tahini Party Plate (page 85)

Eggplant Schnitzel with Spiced Harissa Tomato Sauce and Garlicky Tahini (page 179)

Ultimate Shroom Shawarma (page 180)

Root Steaks with Chilichurri (page 184)

Squash and Walnut Kibbeh with Tahini, Sumac, and Lemon (page 191)

Arayes: Lebanese Stuffed Pitas with Cauliflower, Mushrooms, and Walnuts (page 193)

Smoky Shakshuka Sandies (page 217)

The Greenest Falafel (page 259)

spicy green tahini

terracotta tahini

garlicky tahini

baked feta and olives with citrus

½ cup pitted or whole
Castelvetrano olives

½ cup pitted or whole Kalamata
olives

5 fresh oregano sprigs

1½ tablespoons fennel seeds

Zest of ½ orange

1 medium fresh cayenne chile,
sliced

1 pound Greek feta, drained and
patted dry with a paper towel

¼ cup extra-virgin olive oil

2 tablespoons honey

Flaky sea salt, for serving

Good crusty bread, for serving

This is the ultimate party-starter. You can toss together all the ingredients ahead of time, then throw it in the oven just before your guests arrive. Right when everyone's getting their first glass of cold, crisp wine, you'll be right there with this bubbling dish of sweet-salty creaminess waiting to be swabbed up with good fresh bread. And because every bite is different with all the olives, herbs, citrus, and honey, you can pretty much bet that everyone's going back for more until it's completely demolished.

SCHMEAR IT ON . . .

1. Position the top oven rack about 6 inches under the broiler. Preheat the oven to 400°F.

2. In a small baking dish, combine the olives, oregano, fennel, orange zest, and chile. Nestle the feta in the middle and drizzle everything with the olive oil.

3. Bake until the feta and olives have softened, about 20 minutes. Set the oven to broil and broil for 3 to 5 minutes, until golden on top.

4. Drizzle with the honey and sprinkle with flaky salt. Serve with bread.

Herby Olive Oil Challah (page 228)

Jerusalem Bagel Dinner Rolls
(page 232)

Laffa Two Ways (page 236)

condiments, dips, and all the noshes

lemon-braised leek and chickpea masabacha

Serves 4 to 6

1 (15-ounce) can chickpeas, drained and rinsed

½ teaspoon baking soda

3 tablespoons extra-virgin olive oil, plus more for serving

3 medium leeks, ends trimmed, dark green leaves removed, sliced halfway through and rinsed then sliced into ½-inch-thick rings

Kosher salt to taste

Juice of 1 lemon, plus more to taste

¾ cup Garlicky Tahini (page 59), plus more for drizzling

You'll find this rustic version of hummus across the Levant. *Masabacha* means "swimming" in Arabic, as in chickpeas swimming in tahini and lemon (pretty much my fantasy afternoon). Adding sweet caramelized leeks makes it a really festive, deeply satisfying dip or whole-meal situation.

1. In a medium pot, combine the chickpeas and baking soda with 2 cups of water. Bring to a boil over medium-high heat, then reduce the heat to low and let simmer until the chickpeas are tender, 15 to 20 minutes.

2. While the chickpeas boil, heat the olive oil in a large nonstick pan with a fitted lid over medium heat. When the oil shimmers, add the leeks, season with a good pinch of salt, and allow them to sear without stirring until golden on the first side, 6 to 8 minutes. Flip and repeat for another 3 to 4 minutes.

3. Add the lemon juice and ½ cup of water and cover. Reduce the heat to low and let the leeks simmer until tender, about 20 minutes. Remove the lid and continue simmering until most of the liquid has

cooked off, about 3 minutes. Remove the pan from the heat.

4. Drain the chickpeas and give them a good shake in the strainer to help remove some of the skins.

5. Add the chickpeas to a medium bowl with the garlicky tahini. Use a fork to mash until the mixture is well combined but still chunky. Add half of the braised leeks (I like using the ones that are no longer perfect little rings) and mix well. Season with a little more lemon juice and salt to wake up the flavors, if desired.

6. Spoon the masabacha into a serving dish and carefully arrange the remaining braised leeks on top. Drizzle with more garlicky tahini, a glug of olive oil, and a squeeze of lemon.

SCHMEAR IT ON . . .

Herby Olive Oil Challah (page 228)

Jerusalem Bagel Dinner Rolls (page 232)

Laffa Two Ways (page 236)

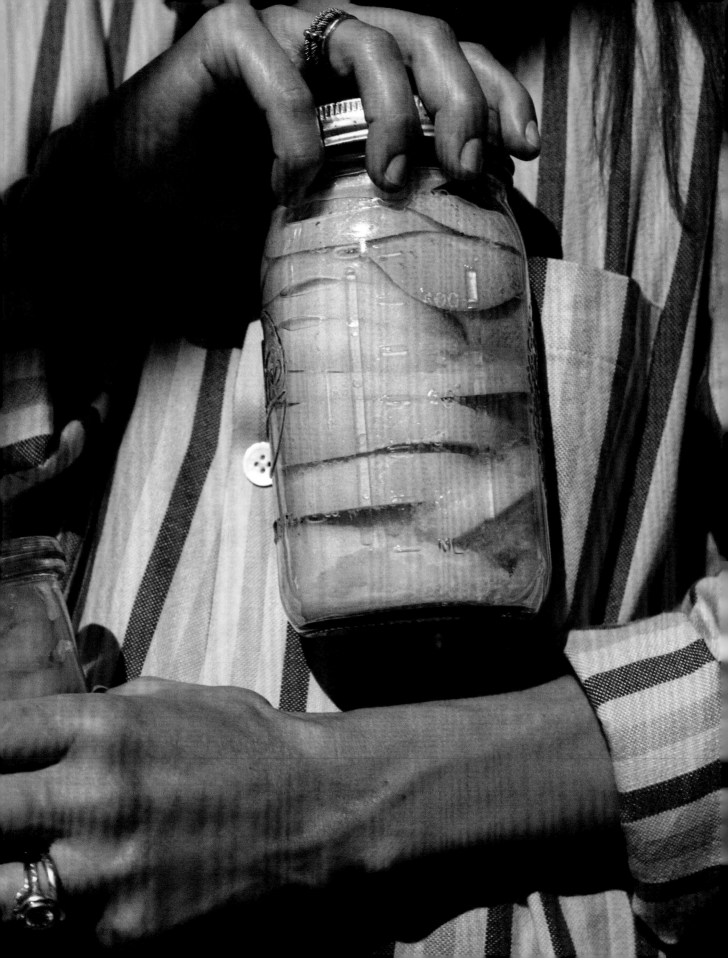

preserved lemons two ways

I did it. I figured out how to make the ultimate preserved lemons in under an hour. That's a huge deal not only because this process normally takes a lot longer—and finding them in the store is not always a sure thing—but also because, along with tahini, preserved lemon is one of those ingredients that I cannot stop reaching for in the kitchen. The lemony, salty, pickle-y pop makes any dish so much more exciting, and now, thanks to these two pared-down versions—one a still-traditional shortcut, the other a full-on cheat—you can have on-demand preserved lemons whenever you need them. The traditional-ish method calls for slicing the lemons first, then rubbing them in salt, which helps the cure do its thing faster. The need-it-now method involves boiling the lemons, which softens their skin and speeds up how quickly they soak up the salt. Either way, make sure you rinse the rinds before using them!

the traditional-ish way

MAKES 6 PRESERVED LEMONS

6 lemons, scrubbed clean and sliced ¼ inch thick, plus the juice of 2 lemons, as needed

6 tablespoons kosher salt

1 tablespoon Aleppo pepper or red chile flakes (optional)

1. Bring a large pot of water to a boil over high heat. Add a 16-ounce glass jar and its lid and boil for 10 minutes. Use tongs to carefully remove the jar and lid and allow them to steam dry while you start the lemons.

2. In a medium bowl, toss the lemon slices with the salt and Aleppo (if using). Allow the lemons to sit at room temperature, covered, for 30 minutes before stacking

recipes continue

condiments, dips, and all the noshes

them in the sterilized jar and pouring over any lemon juice and salt that's settled at the bottom of the bowl. If the lemons are not fully submerged in juice, add more fresh lemon juice.

3. Tightly seal the jar and store at room temperature for up to 3 days, then store in the fridge for up to 3 months. Be sure to rinse the lemons to remove some of the salt before using them.

the need-it-now way

MAKES 2 PRESERVED LEMONS

2 lemons, scrubbed clean and sliced ¼ inch thick

2 tablespoons kosher salt

1. Bring a large pot of water to a boil over high heat. Add an 8-ounce glass jar and its lid and boil for 10 minutes. Use tongs to carefully remove the jar and lid and allow them to steam dry while you start the lemons.

2. In the same pot, bring 6 cups of water to a boil over high heat. Add the lemon slices and reduce the heat to medium. Simmer for 15 minutes; you want the rinds to be soft.

3. Drain the lemons and allow them to steam dry in the colander or sieve. Transfer the lemons to a large bowl and toss with the salt. Layer the salted lemons in the sterilized jar, giving them a gentle nudge so they all fit. (Smooshing them a bit so they release some of their juices is not a bad thing.)

4. Tightly seal the jar and store at room temperature. You can use the lemons after 30 minutes, but I recommend waiting at least 3 hours.

5. Store the lemons at room temperature for up to 3 days, then store in the fridge for up to 3 months. Be sure to rinse the lemons to remove some of the salt before using them.

sticky jammy eggplant

FOR THE EGGPLANT

3 medium eggplants

Kosher salt to taste

Extra-virgin olive oil

FOR THE SAUCE

¼ cup extra-virgin olive oil

6 medium shallots, sliced

1 teaspoon kosher salt,
plus more to taste

1 teaspoon cumin seeds

1 teaspoon paprika

Pinch of ground cinnamon

Freshly ground black pepper
to taste

3 medium garlic cloves, sliced

⅓ cup tomato paste

1 tablespoon Fast 'n' Fresh
Harissa (page 33)

1 teaspoon honey

1 teaspoon pomegranate
molasses (see page 24), or juice
of ½ lemon

Eggplant is my love language. I love how custardy the veg gets when it's cooked down, and if it's charred on the grill first and infused with all that smoke? Forget it. When I sit down for a dinner of kebabs and salatim, my first order of business is getting all up in the eggplant dips and salads. There's typically some kind of spread where eggplant has been simmered in a tomato-based sauce so it's got that balancing brightness and acidity, plus the signature red grease from paprika and olive oil that is the universal sign for deliciousness. This dish is my re-creation of the latter, and is meant to be paired with creamier spreads for balance, schmeared on bread as is or as a sandwich base, or enjoyed on its own as a cold salad, especially if you keep it in the fridge for a few days, which you absolutely should. Is it the sexiest dish you'll ever make? Probably not. But it's definitely going to be one of the tastiest.

1. Preheat the oven to 425°F.

2. Make the eggplant: Trim the ends of each eggplant, peel, and slice lengthwise into thirds. Then slice each long piece lengthwise again into thirds (so you have long spears). Arrange the eggplant slices on a baking sheet and season with salt. Allow the eggplant to sit for 10 to 15 minutes, then thoroughly pat dry with paper towels.

3. Wipe the baking sheet dry and line with parchment paper. Arrange the eggplant in a single layer, drizzle with enough olive oil to coat well, and season with a healthy pinch of salt. Roast for 35 to 45 minutes, until golden all over.

4. While the eggplant roasts, make the sauce: Heat the olive oil in a large skillet with a fitted lid over medium heat. When

recipe continues

condiments, dips, and all the noshes

the oil shimmers, add the shallots, salt, cumin, paprika, cinnamon, and a few cracks of pepper. Sauté, stirring occasionally, until the shallots are translucent and beginning to brown, about 15 minutes.

5. Add the garlic and sauté just until fragrant, about 1 minute. Stir in the tomato paste and harissa and cook until the mixture is a dark, rusty red, about 1 minute. Add 1 cup of water plus the honey and pomegranate molasses and stir to combine.

6. Let the sauce come to a simmer, then cover and reduce the heat to medium-low. Cook until the mixture is sticky and delish, about 20 minutes. Season with more salt if needed and add the roasted eggplant. Toss to coat, cover, and cook just long enough for the eggplant to absorb the sauce, 1 to 2 minutes more.

7. Serve warm or cold. Store in a sealed container in the fridge for up to 1 week.

tzatziki with crispy shallots

Serves 4 to 6 (makes 2½ cups)

2 large Persian or mini cucumbers

2 cups full-fat Greek yogurt

⅓ cup chopped fresh dill,
plus more for serving

Grated zest and juice of ½ lemon

1 medium garlic clove, grated

¾ teaspoon kosher salt,
plus more to taste

2 medium shallots, thinly sliced

2 teaspoons cornstarch

¼ cup extra-virgin olive oil,
plus more for serving

Flaky sea salt, for serving

Laffa (page 236), Challah
(page 228), pita, or other good
bread, for serving (optional)

SCHMEAR IT ON...

Grilled Romano Beans with
Walnuts and Tzatziki (page 163)

Charred Beets with Honey
Caraway Lentils and Tzatziki
(page 183)

Tzatziki is one of my favorite dips/condiments: it's tangy, it's herbaceous—what's not to love? I also tend to reach for it a lot in my cooking, since classic Mediterranean and Middle Eastern flavors just vibe together—probably because they share a backyard and so many of the same ingredients. Tzatziki also happens to be the perfect spread for bringing together a veg dish. Finished with crispy shallots for just the right amount of bite, this is almost impossible not to devour in one sitting.

1. On the medium holes of a box grater, grate the cucumbers. Use your hands to squeeze out as much juice as possible. You could also use a cheesecloth. (I encourage you to drink the juice like a shot—so fresh.)

2. In a medium bowl, stir together the yogurt, cucumber, dill, lemon juice, garlic, and salt. Season with more salt, if desired, and set aside.

3. In a medium bowl, toss the shallots with the cornstarch, making sure to separate the individual shallot rings and coat each one well.

4. Heat the olive oil in a large skillet over medium heat. When the oil shimmers, increase the heat to medium-high and add the shallots. Fry, stirring constantly so the shallots don't burn, until they are golden and crispy, 2 to 3 minutes. Use a slotted spoon or a kitchen spider to transfer the shallots to a paper towel–lined plate. Immediately sprinkle them with a good pinch of salt.

5. To serve, spread the dip over a serving plate and press the back of a large spoon in the center to make a pretty swirl. Top with the crispy shallots, drizzle with olive oil, and sprinkle with dill, lemon zest, and flaky salt.

6. Serve with laffa, challah, or pita or eat on its own with a spoon. It's that good.

condiments, dips, and all the noshes

spicy pepper dip with walnuts and pomegranate molasses

Makes about 2 cups

3 medium red bell peppers

2 slices good crusty bread

1 medium shallot, peeled and halved

1 small jalapeño or fresh cayenne, long-hot, or serrano chile (depending on what you have and how much heat you like)

¼ cup extra-virgin olive oil, plus more for serving

½ cup raw walnuts, toasted in a dry pan until fragrant and chopped

1 medium garlic clove

1 teaspoon kosher salt, plus more to taste

Pomegranate molasses (see page 24), for serving

Flaky sea salt, for serving

Challah (page 228), Laffa (page 236), or other fresh bread, for serving

This is my spin on muhammara, a Syrian roasty red pepper spread that gets meaty earthiness from walnuts and toasted bread. But the best part is how easy it is to make: You throw almost everything on the grill for a hit of smoke and char, then blitz it up to make this ridiculous umami-fied condiment. To round out the flavors, I add a drizzle of tart pomegranate molasses. Trust me on this one—it makes it all pop.

1. Preheat a grill or grill pan to medium-high heat.

2. In a large bowl, combine the bell peppers, bread, shallot, and jalapeño. Drizzle with the olive oil and toss to coat. Arrange everything on the grill or grill pan (you might need to work in batches) and grill until the bread is nicely charred, about 2 minutes per side. Remove the bread and continue grilling, covered, until the vegetables are deeply charred and tender, rotating so they cook evenly, about 10 minutes total.

3. Add the bell peppers and jalapeño to a large bowl. Cover with a towel or large plate and allow them to steam for about 10 minutes. Meanwhile, roughly chop the bread and add it to a food processor along with the shallot, ¼ cup of the walnuts, the garlic, and salt. Set aside.

4. When the bell peppers and jalapeño are cool enough to handle, slip off and discard their skins. Discard the stems and seeds as well. Tear the peppers into chunky pieces and add them to the food processor. Blend until uniform and chunky-smooth. Season with more salt, if needed.

5. Spread the dip over a serving plate and sprinkle with the remaining ¼ cup walnuts. Drizzle with olive oil and pomegranate molasses and finish with a pinch of flaky salt. Serve with plenty of fresh bread for dipping.

SCHMEAR IT ON . . .

Herby Olive Oil Challah (page 228)

Jerusalem Bagel Dinner Rolls (page 232)

Laffa Two Ways (page 236)

tahini baby

cabbage salad with sumac and dill

Serves 4 to 6

FOR THE DRESSING

¼ cup extra-virgin olive oil

2 tablespoons red wine vinegar

Grated zest and juice of 1 lemon

1 tablespoon ground sumac, plus more for serving

1 tablespoon honey

2 teaspoons kosher salt

½ medium garlic clove, grated

FOR THE SALAD

½ medium head red cabbage, halved and finely sliced

½ cup chopped fresh dill

⅓ cup roasted salted sunflower seeds

⅓ cup dried fruit, such as raisins, currants, or cranberries (optional)

There's an unwritten rule that when you put together a spread of salatim—or when you're stuffing a pita—you've got to have at least one great crunchy, vinegary cabbage salad. Well, this is exactly that . . . times ten. It has the simplicity of a slaw but with the added salad-y sex appeal of crunchy sunflower seeds, fresh dill, and citrusy sumac vin. Add dried fruit if you're feeling cray; serve it as a side salad or as a condiment; enjoy it the day it's made or the day after. You cannot go wrong.

1. **Make the dressing:** In a medium bowl, whisk together the olive oil, vinegar, lemon zest and juice, sumac, honey, salt, and garlic. Set aside.

2. **Make the salad:** In a serving bowl, toss together the cabbage, dill, sunflower seeds, and dried fruit (if using). Pour the vinaigrette over the salad and give another toss to mix well. Sprinkle with a bit more sumac and serve.

3. Store in a sealed container in the fridge for up to 3 days.

charred pepper salad with preserved lemons and scallion drizzle

Serves 4

5 medium red, yellow, or orange bell peppers (or a mix of all three)

3 scallions, trimmed and sliced (white and green parts)

¼ cup extra-virgin olive oil

1 tablespoon finely chopped rinsed rind of Preserved Lemons (page 67)

2 teaspoons red wine vinegar

1 small garlic clove, grated

½ teaspoon kosher salt

Freshly ground black pepper to taste

Handful of torn fresh cilantro leaves (about ⅓ cup; see Note)

Flaky sea salt, for serving

Note: I can already hear the cilantro haters out there asking if they can sub it out and the answer is yes; you can use parsley instead. But when the love for cilantro is real, the love runs deep, and some dishes are just meant to have cilantro. That's all I'm going to say about it.

The second the weather turns warm—and most of the winter, too, who are we kidding—I'm thinking about grilling peppers, then marinating them in a preserved lemon vinaigrette packed with sweet-heat scallions for a bright, tangy salad, condiment, or side. This is also a great mezze served with more grilled vegetables to give them some much-needed brightness and acidity, or just keep it in the fridge and scoop it onto salads, grains, sandwiches, or any other dish that needs a little pick-me-up.

1. Using a gas stovetop, grill on high heat, or broiler on high and a pair of long tongs, char the peppers until they're fully blackened and blistered all over, about 10 minutes. Place the charred peppers in a large bowl and cover with a towel. Let the peppers steam for 20 minutes.

2. When the peppers are cool enough to handle, slip off the skins and remove the cores and discard. Slice the peppers into bite-size chunks and set aside.

3. In a small bowl, toss together the scallions, olive oil, preserved lemon, vinegar, garlic, salt, and a few cracks of black pepper.

4. Spread the peppers over a serving plate or bowl and drizzle the scallion mixture over the top. Sprinkle with the cilantro and the flaky salt and serve.

5. Store leftovers in a sealed container in the fridge for up to 3 days.

roasted honey aleppo cherry tomatoes with labaneh

Makes about 2 cups

4 cups cherry tomatoes
(I like buying them on the
vine and baking them with
the stems attached)

⅓ cup extra-virgin olive oil,
plus more for serving

1 tablespoon honey

2 teaspoons Aleppo pepper
or red chile flakes, plus more
for serving

1 teaspoon kosher salt

Freshly ground black pepper
to taste

1 cup Labaneh (page 42)

Warm Laffa (page 236),
Challah (page 228), pita, or
other warm bread, for serving

Cherry tomatoes, whether they're braised, roasted, grilled, or eaten straight out of the container, will always be one of my all-time favorite veg (fruit?), and they will always make a dish better with their sweet acidity. To really dial that up to a ten, I let them roast until they've submitted to jammy, caramelized, charred oblivion and highlight all that natural sweetness with honey and a little heat from Aleppo. Spooned over a bed of labaneh, this would very much be at home on the table as a condiment with a bunch of veg and grains or served on its own with bread.

1. Preheat the oven to 425°F.

2. Arrange the tomatoes on a baking sheet. Pour the olive oil and honey over the top and sprinkle with the Aleppo, salt, and a few cracks of black pepper. Toss until just combined.

3. Roast for 30 to 35 minutes, until the tomatoes have gotten nice, deep color and have completely deflated.

4. Spread the labaneh over a serving plate and place the tomatoes over the top. Finish with another sprinkle of Aleppo and drizzle of olive oil. Serve with warm bread.

5. Store leftovers in a sealed container in the fridge for up to 2 days.

whipped feta with crispy herbs and honey

Serves 4

1 cup drained, crumbled sheep's milk feta

½ cup Labaneh (page 42) or full-fat Greek yogurt

3 tablespoons extra-virgin olive oil

5 fresh oregano sprigs

5 fresh sage leaves

Grated zest from ½ lemon

1 tablespoon honey

Freshly ground black pepper to taste

Feta is just one of those cheeses that I'm always looking for excuses to eat more of—it's salty, it's briny, and it's a huge crowd-pleaser. Especially when you whip it into a creamy cloud of a dip with labaneh and finish it off with crisped oregano and sage, a drizzle of honey, bright lemon zest, and just a tiny hit of heat from black pepper. People. Lose. Their. Minds. Once they try to wrap their heads around how beyond delicious it is, they really can't handle how something so simple can taste so complex. It's the kind of dish that doesn't need anything more than some good challah, laffa, or sourdough, but it's also just the thing for heaping veg over too.

1. In a blender, combine the feta, labaneh, and 1 tablespoon of the olive oil. Pulse until just combined (take care not to overwhip here).

2. Spread the mixture over the bottom of a shallow serving bowl or plate and set aside.

3. Heat the remaining 2 tablespoons olive oil in a medium skillet over medium heat. When the oil shimmers, add the sprigs of oregano and sage. Fry the herbs for just a couple seconds, then remove the pan from the heat. Set aside for the oil and herbs to cool, about 5 minutes.

4. Top the whipped feta with the fried herbs and lemon zest, drizzle with the honey and some of the herby oil, and finish with a couple cracks of pepper.

SCHMEAR IT ON...

Crispy and Light Zucchini Chive Patties with Honey and Labaneh (page 98)

Corn Tartines with Aleppo Butter and Nectarines (page 210)

Herby Olive Oil Challah (page 228)

Laffa Two Ways (page 236)

tahini party plate

Small handful of your favorite chiles (I like long-hots, serranos, and jalapeños)

1 cup Garlicky Tahini (page 59)

¼ cup Grated Tomato for Everything (page 38)

¼ cup Celery Zhoug (page 30; see Note)

¼ cup Preserved Lemon Toum (page 41; see Note)

Extra-virgin olive oil, for serving

Flaky sea salt, for serving

Laffa (page 236), Herby Olive Oil Challah (page 228), or Jerusalem Bagels (page 232), for serving

Note: Don't feel like you have to be locked in to these specific condiments! I sometimes switch out zhoug for harissa or toum for amba pepper sauce—there's just too many dips and too little time.

Condiment load-UP; that is what I'm talking about. You'll find a version of this all-star dip-condiment lineup at so many different restaurants in Tel Aviv. A real standout for me is at Port Sa'id, one of my favorite restaurants there, where the chef Eyal Shani layers so many different condiments and hot sauces for dipping and dunking. I was so inspired by this ultimate way to serve some of my favorite flavors and textures together. The objective here is to take whatever fresh bread you have on hand and literally drag it through everything to get the perfect bite. Rich, nutty, tangy, spicy, magic.

1. On a hot grill or grill pan, char the chiles on all sides, 1 to 2 minutes per side. Remove from the heat and set aside.

2. Spread the tahini over a small serving plate. On one corner, mound the grated tomato. On the opposite side, dollop the zhoug, then nestle the chiles into the mix. Add a third mound of the toum. Drizzle with olive oil, sprinkle with salt, and drag your bread through the whole mess.

condiments, dips, and all the noshes

brekky and brunch

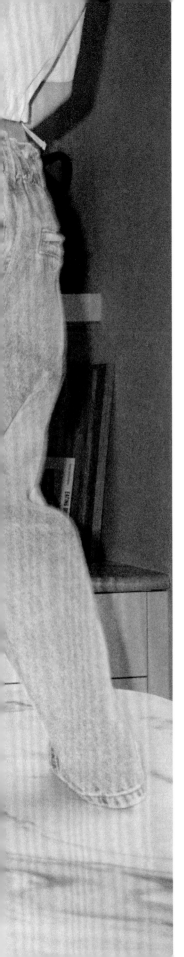

When I think about what I want in a breakfast dish, my first question is: *Can I make this pre-coffee with two children climbing on me and an entire day's to-do list knocking around my brain?* And for brunch it's basically that plus *Will it feed a thousand (or eight) people?* Luckily, I've spent time honing a stash of **go-to recipes** that are less about technique and hands-on time and much more about solid flavor combinations. There's a little fry here and chop there, but mainly you're throwing a bunch of things into a pan or baking dish and letting time, heat, and the ingredients themselves do the rest. They're dishes that are built for **simplicity and also durability**—show me something more delicious than a slab of Asparagus, Feta, and Za'atar Frittata or Swiss Chard, Oregano, and Dill Phyllo Tart or Cardamom Apricot Upside-Down Olive Oil Cake that you've been picking at all week. And if all else fails, you can just schmear some labaneh on toast—maybe with a sprinkle of Fennel Seed Pistachio Dukkah—and call it a day.

dukkah toast

1½ cups Labaneh (page 42) or full-fat Greek yogurt

4 slices your favorite bread (I like sourdough for this), toasted if not day-of fresh

¼ cup Fennel Seed Pistachio Dukkah (recipe follows)

Extra-virgin olive oil, for serving

Honey, for serving (optional)

It's hard to even call this a recipe, but it would be a crime to not tell you that this combination is great on toast as an easy breakfast option. Dukkah is a nutty, seedy blend with mellow spices that lends instant flavor and texture to anything it's sprinkled on, and it is a staple in my fridge for elevating a dish in need. So when time, groceries, or inspiration runs a little low for breakfast, I need only grab whatever bread I happen to have, a labaneh ball from the jar on my counter, and a healthy pinch of dukkah to make something legit worthy of serving to guests. This recipe is genius in its simplicity, but you could also dress it up with a drizzle of honey or even a dusting of lemon zest to bring some citrus flavor.

Spread the labaneh over each slice of bread. Sprinkle with the dukkah and finish with a drizzle of olive oil and, if you're feeling like a little something sweet, some honey too.

recipe continues

tahini baby

fennel seed pistachio dukkah

MAKES 1½ CUPS

¼ cup sesame seeds

1½ tablespoons fennel seeds

1 teaspoon coriander seeds

¼ cup raw pumpkin seeds

¼ cup raw sunflower seeds

½ cup roasted salted pistachios

¾ teaspoon kosher salt

½ teaspoon ground cardamom

1. In a small skillet over medium-low heat, toast the sesame, fennel, and coriander seeds until lightly golden, about 2 minutes. Transfer the seeds to a bowl and set aside.

2. In the same pan over medium-low heat, add the pumpkin and sunflower seeds and toast until lightly golden, about 2 minutes. Remove the pan from the heat.

3. In a food processor or high-speed blender, combine the pistachios with the toasted pumpkin and sunflower seeds. Pulse until just broken down.

4. Transfer the mixture to a container with a fitted lid and add the toasted sesame, fennel, and coriander seeds plus the salt and cardamom. Mix with a spoon and cover.

5. Store in a sealed container in the fridge for up to 2 weeks.

eggplant, cherry tomato, and sage galette

Serves 6 to 8

1 (8-ounce) ball fresh mozzarella

⅓ cup roughly crumbled Parmesan

⅓ cup extra-virgin olive oil, plus more for brushing

1 small eggplant, chopped into 1-inch pieces

Kosher salt to taste

1 medium garlic clove, finely chopped

All-purpose flour, for dusting (optional)

2 sheets puff pastry (from a 1-pound box)

1 cup cherry tomatoes, halved

Handful of fresh sage leaves

1 large egg

2 tablespoons sesame seeds

Flaky sea salt, for sprinkling

I learned young that there is nothing like succulent, juicy roast veg and earthy fresh herbs tucked inside a buttery, flaky crust.

When the time came to make my own version, though, I had to stand up for what is right—and that meant not making a dough from scratch. Because when you add gorgeous layers of eggplant and tomato and mozzarella and sage to store-bought puff pastry, you still end up with a brunch centerpiece that's just the right amount of fancy. Oh, but that doesn't mean you need to fuck around with silverware for this—get up in there with your hands.

Serve this with a simple salad or any of your favorite dips.

1. Preheat the oven to 400°F. Line a baking sheet with parchment paper.

2. In a food processor, combine the mozzarella and Parmesan and give them a nice whiz until they're completely broken down. Set aside.

3. Heat the olive oil in a large skillet over medium-low heat. When the oil shimmers, add the eggplant and a good pinch of salt. Sauté, stirring occasionally, until the eggplant is golden brown, about 15 minutes. Add the garlic and sauté just until fragrant, about 10 seconds

longer. Remove the pan from the heat and set aside.

4. On a lightly floured work surface or on a silicone baking mat, adjoin the short edges of the puff pastry and use a rolling pin to roll out the sheets into a 14 × 15-inch rectangle that is ¼ inch thick. If you want, at this point you can trim the corners to make the galette circular—both shapes are equally perfect and delicious.

5. Carefully transfer the dough to the prepared baking sheet. Sprinkle the cheese evenly

recipe continues

over the dough, leaving a ½-inch border around the edge. Scatter the eggplant over the cheese and dot with the tomatoes, cut side up. Sprinkle the sage evenly over the top.

6. In a small bowl, use a fork to beat the egg with 1 tablespoon of water.

7. Carefully fold the edges of the pastry over the filling. Brush the egg wash over the crust and sprinkle with the sesame seeds. Brush the top of the tart with olive oil and sprinkle with a good pinch of flaky salt. Bake for 35 to 45 minutes, until the crust is golden and the cheese is bubbly.

8. Slice and serve. Store leftovers in the fridge for up to 5 days, and reheat in the oven before serving.

cheddar scallion matzo brei with zhoug and za'atar

Serves 2

FOR THE MATZO BREI

4 large eggs, beaten

Kosher salt and freshly ground black pepper to taste

3 sheets matzo

4 tablespoons (½ stick) salted butter

2 scallions, trimmed and thinly sliced (white and green parts)

¼ cup grated cheddar

FOR SERVING

Pinch of Za'atar (page 25)

Extra-virgin olive oil

Celery Zhoug (page 30)

Grated Tomato for Everything (page 38)

Most people of the Passover persuasion will make matzo brei (rhymes with "try") around the holiday, which is basically eggs scrambled with matzo, or unleavened cracker heaven that tastes and smells a little bit like the box it comes in but in a good way—don't ask me why. But my family and I make it year-round because we're obsessed with how it takes a regular egg dish to a more interesting, satisfying place—especially this fluffy, super-cheesy, souped-up version.

1. **Make the matzo brei:** In a small bowl, beat the eggs and season with salt and pepper.

2. Soak the matzo in warm water for 10 seconds just to soften slightly. Break the matzo into bite-size pieces and set aside.

3. Melt 2 tablespoons of the butter in a large skillet over medium heat. Add the matzo and cook, stirring a bit as it toasts, 3 to 5 minutes. Sprinkle in most of the scallions, reserving some for garnish. Sauté, stirring, until the scallions have softened, 3 to 5 minutes.

4. Reduce the heat to medium-low and transfer half of the matzo mixture to a bowl. Add the remaining 2 tablespoons butter to the skillet. When the butter has melted, add the egg mixture and sprinkle with the cheese. When the eggs start to set around the edges, 1 to 2 minutes, use a spatula to gently fold the mixture to evenly distribute the matzo. Add the remaining matzo and continue to fold it in until the eggs are just set, about 1 minute more.

5. **To serve:** Top with a juicy pinch of za'atar, a drizzle of olive oil, and the reserved scallions and serve with zhoug and grated tomato.

brekky and brunch

97

crispy and light zucchini chive patties with honey and labaneh

Serves 4 to 6 (makes 10 patties)

4 medium zucchini

3 teaspoons kosher salt, plus more to taste

½ cup all-purpose flour

⅓ cup chopped fresh chives

¼ cup chopped fresh dill or mint, plus more for garnish

2 large eggs

2 large garlic cloves, grated

½ teaspoon ground cumin

½ teaspoon ground coriander

½ teaspoon freshly ground black pepper

¾ cup panko bread crumbs, plus more as needed

¾ cup refined avocado oil or any neutral oil you like to fry with

Labaneh (page 42), Whipped Feta (page 82), or full-fat Greek yogurt, for serving

Grated zest of 1 lemon, for serving

2 to 3 tablespoons honey, for serving

I love a savory fritter option for breakfast or brunch, and it's never made sense to me that potatoes get all the love. Zucchini lends itself well to a fritter and feels nice and light, and because it's so mild in flavor, it's a delicious canvas for letting fresh herbs like chives and dill and spices like cumin and coriander shine. With a panko coating that guarantees a light, airy middle and a crispy, crunchy exterior, these are still refreshingly low-key to assemble. The surprising honey finish and cool, creamy labaneh also make them perfect for a schmancy brunch.

1. Line a large bowl with cheesecloth or a kitchen towel.

2. On the large holes of a box grater, grate the zucchini into the bowl. Sprinkle with 1½ teaspoons of the salt and let the zucchini sit for 15 minutes to release its liquid. Gather up the edges of the cheesecloth or towel and squeeze out as much liquid as possible. (Your extra-crispy patties will thank you for it.)

3. In a large bowl, combine the zucchini with the flour, chives, dill, eggs, garlic, the remaining 1½ teaspoons salt, the cumin, coriander, and pepper. Mix well.

4. Preheat the oven to 200°F. Line a cooling rack with paper towels. Spread the panko over a large plate.

5. Heat the oil in a large pan over medium-high heat. When the oil shimmers, scoop ¼ cup of the zucchini mixture, pack it tightly in your hand to form a patty, and gently roll it in the panko to coat.

6. Add the patty to the pan and gently press the top with a spatula. Fry until golden, 2 to 3 minutes. Flip and continue cooking until golden on the second side, 2 to 3 more minutes. Transfer the patty to

the paper towel–lined cooling rack and immediately sprinkle it with salt. Place the patty on a baking sheet and keep in the warm oven until ready to serve. Repeat with the remaining zucchini mixture.

7. When ready to serve, spread the labaneh over a serving plate and top with the patties, or serve it on the side for schmearing. Sprinkle with the lemon zest and drizzle with the honey. Serve hot.

lebanese breakfast sandy

Serves 2

½ cup Labaneh (page 42) or full-fat Greek yogurt

2 Sesame Laffa (page 236)

3 teaspoons Za'atar (page 25)

2 medium Persian or mini cucumbers, thinly sliced

9 medium radishes, thinly sliced (optional)

2 handfuls of fresh parsley leaves

2 tablespoons extra-virgin olive oil

Flaky sea salt, for serving

Celery Zhoug (page 30) or sliced hot green chiles, for serving (optional)

I had a version of this sandwich when I was shooting the very first episode of *Eden Eats* for the Cooking Channel. We were in Austin, Texas, and we were profiling a pita bakery run by a Lebanese family. Not only did they feed me the most beautifully fluffy pita straight out of the oven, but they also layered it with cold, creamy labaneh, fresh tomato, and za'atar (which, with its wild oregano and sesame seeds, is a classic combo with labaneh). To say it was heavenly is a major understatement; to this day, it's a flavor combination that I go back to over and over again. So it only makes sense that I would come up with my own version of this loaded yet light-feeling breakfast sandwich, which is perfect for packing up and taking out the door with you. It's a weekday no-brainer.

Schmear ¼ cup of the labaneh over each laffa. Sprinkle each with half of the za'atar and scatter the cucumbers and radishes (if using) over the top. Finish each with a small handful of parsley, a drizzle of half the olive oil, and a sprinkle of flaky salt. Wrap and eat with dollops of zhoug or green chile slices, if desired.

swiss chard, oregano, and dill phyllo tart

Makes one 9-inch tart (serves 6 to 8)

¼ cup plus 2 tablespoons
extra-virgin olive oil

1 small yellow onion,
finely chopped

Kosher salt and freshly ground
black pepper to taste

1 bunch Swiss chard
(6 to 8 leaves), ribs removed
and thinly sliced

3 medium garlic cloves,
finely chopped

½ teaspoon ground coriander

8 phyllo dough sheets, thawed

6 large eggs

1 cup heavy cream

¼ cup whole milk

⅓ cup finely chopped fresh dill

1 cup crumbled sheep's milk feta

½ cup Gruyère chunks, plus more
for grating

4 fresh oregano sprigs

I like to think of this tart as an open-faced spanakopita, or a big, beautiful mound of cooked greens scented with dill and oregano and balanced with briny feta and nutty Gruyère, all heaped on top of a rustic phyllo dough crust. It's the perfect lazy Sunday tart to bake up and serve with a salad and plenty of tzatziki (page 73).

1. Preheat the oven to 350°F.

2. Heat 2 tablespoons of the olive oil in a large skillet over medium heat. When the oil shimmers, add the onion and season with salt and pepper. Sauté, stirring occasionally, until translucent and golden in some places, 5 to 7 minutes.

3. Add the Swiss chard and season again with salt and pepper. Add the garlic and coriander, stir to combine, and reduce the heat to medium-low. Cook, stirring occasionally, until the chard is tender and the liquid has cooked off, 2 to 3 minutes. Remove from the heat and set aside to cool while you finish assembling the tart.

4. With the remaining ¼ cup olive oil, brush each sheet of phyllo dough and layer them

in a 9-inch cake or pie pan. You'll have overhanging edges and that's okay; we're going for rustic. Set aside.

5. In a large bowl, whisk together the eggs, cream, milk, dill, 1 teaspoon of salt, and ½ teaspoon of pepper. Add the chard mixture, crumble in the feta and Gruyère, and mix well. Pour the mixture over the phyllo and finish with a scattering of the oregano sprigs and more Gruyère grated over the top.

6. Bake for 45 to 55 minutes, until the sides of the tart are golden and there is only a little jiggle in the center. Slice and serve.

7. Store leftovers in a sealed container in the fridge for up to 2 days.

lemon ricotta sweet crumb babka

Makes two 9 × 5-inch babkas

FOR THE DOUGH

¾ cup whole milk

¾ cup granulated sugar, plus a pinch

2¼ teaspoons (1 packet) active dry yeast

4½ cups all-purpose flour, plus more for dusting

3 large eggs

1 teaspoon vanilla extract

Grated zest of 1 lemon

8 tablespoons (1 stick) unsalted butter, room temperature, plus more for greasing

1 teaspoon kosher salt

FOR THE FILLING

1 cup ricotta (at least 10% milk fat), room temperature

1 (8-ounce) package plain cream cheese, room temperature

½ cup granulated sugar

2 large egg yolks

Grated zest of 1 lemon

¼ teaspoon vanilla extract

¼ teaspoon kosher salt

FOR THE CRUMB TOPPING AND ASSEMBLY

½ cup granulated sugar

4 tablespoons (½ stick) unsalted butter, plus more for greasing

I like to think that I have sampled almost every single yeasted cake that Israel has to offer—which is a lot—but one of the best that I've ever had was at Milk Bakery in Jaffa. A close friend gave me the insider's tip, but by the time I'd gotten there, the chocolate babka had already sold out. I ordered the sweet cheese version instead, and it completely changed my life. It had a sweet cheese filling bundled up in the softest, fluffiest brioche dough and just a suggestion of citrus to keep it from feeling too one-note. I finally nailed my own recipe at home, and even though it makes two loaves, it all still gets inhaled—for breakfast, for afternoon coffee, for after-school snack, as French toast—before we can even consider freezing one. That said, you could do that, too, and have a just-in-case babka in your freezer.

1. Make the dough: In a small saucepan over medium heat, warm the milk with a pinch of granulated sugar until the milk is almost hot, or just about body temperature, 1 to 2 minutes. (Take care not to let the milk get too hot or it will kill the yeast!) Stir in the yeast and let it bloom for about 5 minutes, until foamy.

2. Transfer the milk mixture to the bowl of a stand mixer fitted with the dough hook. Add the granulated sugar, flour, eggs, vanilla, and lemon zest. Mix on low speed until the dough just begins to come together, about 1 minute. Add the butter and salt and mix again on low speed until the dough is smooth, 15 to 20 minutes.

3. Turn out the dough onto a lightly floured work surface and knead just a couple times to bring the dough together. Grease a large bowl with butter, add the dough, and cover with a damp cloth. Let the dough proof in a warm place

recipe and ingredients continue

¼ cup all-purpose flour

¼ teaspoon kosher salt

1 large egg

Confectioners' sugar

Note: If you don't have two loaf pans, I recommend buying a disposable aluminum one so you can stash the second loaf in the freezer for a rainy day that needs a babka, or give it as a gift. Or you could save half of this dough to use for Pull-Apart Tahini Rugelach (page 277) instead of making two babkas.

for 1½ hours, or until it doubles in size.

4. While the dough proofs, make the filling: Strain the ricotta through a fine-mesh sieve or cheesecloth to remove as much liquid as possible, pressing gently with a rubber spatula. (This will make it a lot easier to assemble the babka.)

5. In a medium bowl, mix together the strained ricotta, cream cheese, granulated sugar, egg yolks, lemon zest, vanilla, and salt.

6. Assemble the babkas: Grease two 9 × 5-inch loaf pans (see Note) with butter and line with parchment paper.

7. Turn out the proofed dough onto a clean work surface. Divide the dough in half and cover the second half with a clean towel. Use a rolling pin to roll out the first half to a ⅛-inch-thick rectangle about 16 × 18 inches. Spread half of the filling mixture over the dough and, starting from the long end, roll the dough tightly. Slice the entire roll down the middle lengthwise so you now have two long strands. Twist the two strands around each other to make one long

braid. Things might get a little (or a lot) messy—that's okay! I promise she'll get her act together after she bakes.

8. Carefully transfer the braid to the loaf pan, cover with a damp towel, and leave it in a warm place to proof for 1½ hours, or until about doubled in size. While it proofs, repeat with the second half of the dough and filling.

9. Preheat the oven to 350°F.

10. While the babkas proof, make the crumb topping: In a small bowl, use your fingers to work together the granulated sugar, butter, flour, and salt until uniform and crumbly.

11. In another small bowl, use a fork to beat the egg with 1 tablespoon of water. Brush both babkas with the egg wash and sprinkle both evenly with the crumb topping.

12. Set the loaf pans on top of a baking sheet and bake for 40 to 50 minutes, until the babkas are golden. If they start to get too dark too quickly, you can cover them with foil.

13. Allow the babkas to cool slightly on a cooling rack before finishing with a nice dusting of confectioners' sugar.

14. Store in a sealed container at room temperature for up to 1 week or wrap in plastic wrap and freeze for up to 1 month.

asparagus, feta, and za'atar frittata

Serves 4 to 6

12 large eggs

¼ cup full-fat Greek yogurt or Labaneh (page 42)

¼ cup whole milk

1 teaspoon kosher salt, plus more to taste

½ teaspoon freshly grated black pepper, plus more to taste

4 tablespoons extra-virgin olive oil

2 tablespoons unsalted butter

1 medium leek, ends trimmed, dark green leaves removed, halved vertically and rinsed then sliced into ½-inch-thick rings

1 bunch asparagus, base peeled, cut into ½-inch pieces (about 2 cups; see Note)

1 medium garlic clove, grated

1 cup crumbled sheep's milk feta

2 tablespoons Za'atar (page 25)

Fresh dill, for garnish

Note: To make this all-season friendly, you could sub roasted squash and/or a hearty green like kale for the asparagus.

Frittatas, like galettes, are your brunching secret weapons. They are meant to be rustic and homey-feeling, which directly translates to unfussy preparation. And that kind of not-trying-too-hard vibe always comes across as effortlessly chic. It also doesn't hurt that a frittata feeds a crowd and can be made ahead, since it's just as good cold or room temp as it is fresh out of the oven. (Which also makes it great as an eat-all-week dish.) I especially love this version, which celebrates spring with bright, salty feta, sweet asparagus, and earthy za'atar.

1. Preheat the oven to 350°F.

2. In a large bowl, whisk together the eggs, yogurt, milk, salt, and pepper. Set aside.

3. Heat 2 tablespoons of the olive oil and the butter in a large ovenproof skillet (I like my 12-inch for this) over medium heat. When the butter has melted and is beginning to foam, add the leek and season with a pinch of salt and pepper. Sauté, stirring occasionally, until translucent, about 4 minutes. Add the asparagus and garlic with another pinch of salt and pepper. Sauté just until the asparagus softens slightly, about 3 minutes.

4. Pour in the egg mixture and give the pan a good shake to mix in the asparagus. Sprinkle the feta evenly over the pan and cook until the edges are just set, about 2 minutes. Carefully transfer the pan to the oven and bake for 10 to 15 minutes, until the middle is just set.

5. While the frittata bakes, mix together the remaining 2 tablespoons olive oil with the za'atar. Drizzle the za'atar oil over the finished frittata and serve immediately, sprinkled with fresh dill.

basbousa pancakes with orange blossom syrup

Serves 4 (makes about 12 pancakes)

FOR THE ORANGE BLOSSOM SYRUP

½ cup sugar

¼ teaspoon orange blossom water (see Note)

1 tablespoon fresh lemon juice (about ½ lemon)

FOR THE PANCAKES

½ cup all-purpose flour

¾ cup semolina

⅓ cup sugar

2 teaspoons baking powder

½ teaspoon kosher salt

¾ cup whole milk

½ cup full-fat Greek yogurt, plus more for serving

4 tablespoons (½ stick) unsalted butter, melted and cooled, plus more for cooking the pancakes

1 large egg

Grated zest of 1 orange, plus more for serving

¼ teaspoon vanilla extract

FOR SERVING

⅓ cup roasted pistachios, finely chopped

As much as I love traditional buttermilk pancakes, let's be honest, they're pretty basic. When I was thinking about how I could give this morning staple a little bit of a Middle Eastern zhuzh, my mind went to basbousa, a syrupy, orange-blossom-water-soaked Egyptian semolina cake. The end result is a piping-hot stack of flapjacks that magically bridge something very familiar with a breakfast or brunch that's much more exciting.

1. **Make the syrup:** In a small saucepan, combine the sugar with ½ cup of water and bring to a simmer over medium heat. Simmer, stirring occasionally, until the sugar has dissolved, about 5 minutes. Turn off the heat and stir in the orange blossom water and lemon juice. Cover to keep warm.

2. Preheat the oven to 200°F.

3. **Make the pancakes:** In a medium bowl, whisk together the flour, semolina, sugar, baking powder, and salt.

4. In a large bowl, whisk together the milk, yogurt, melted butter, egg, orange zest, and vanilla. Add the dry ingredients and whisk until just combined.

5. Melt about 1 tablespoon of butter in a large skillet over medium heat. Add three to four ¼-cup dollops of the batter to the pan and cook until the tops of the pancakes begin to bubble and the edges are golden, about 2 minutes. Flip and cook until the second side is golden, another 2 minutes.

6. Transfer the finished pancakes to a baking sheet and keep them warm in the oven while you repeat with the remaining batter, adding more butter to the pan as needed.

7. **To serve:** Stack the pancakes, sprinkle with the pistachios and orange zest, and pour the warm syrup over the top. Offer with Greek yogurt on the side.

Note: If orange blossom water isn't your thing, or you have trouble finding it (you may need to go to an international market or buy it online), then either leave it out, replace it with a squeeze of lemon juice, or skip the syrup altogether and go with classic maple syrup instead.

cardamom apricot upside-down olive oil cake

Makes one 9-inch cake

FOR THE CARDAMOM APRICOT TOPPING

4 tablespoons (½ stick) unsalted butter, melted, plus more for greasing

½ cup packed light brown sugar

½ teaspoon kosher salt

¼ teaspoon ground cardamom

12 medium apricots, halved and pitted

FOR THE CAKE

1 cup granulated sugar

3 cardamom pods, crushed to remove the seeds

2 cups all-purpose flour

1 teaspoon baking powder

1 teaspoon salt

½ teaspoon baking soda

½ cup extra-virgin olive oil

⅓ cup full-fat Greek yogurt

2 large eggs

1 teaspoon vanilla extract

½ cup whole milk

FOR SERVING

2 tablespoons honey

Full-fat Greek yogurt or Labaneh (page 42)

Meesh mesh is "apricot" in Hebrew, and when meesh mesh season is in full bloom in Israel, you find them in everything from pastries to fruit leathers to spreads. But in North America, apricots are more of an underdog fruit, which I've never really understood, both because of their adorably fuzzy baby-tush softness and also their tart-sweet floral flavor. I particularly like how they cut through the sweetness and richness of a baked good and pair so beautifully with naturally floral spices like cardamom. I've put both to work in this lusciously dense, perfectly breakfast-appropriate cake, which you can leave on your counter and enjoy throughout the day as a snack, with your afternoon coffee or tea, or as dessert.

1. **Make the topping:** Lightly grease a 9-inch cake pan with butter.

2. In a medium bowl, stir together the melted butter, brown sugar, salt, and cardamom. Spread the mixture in an even layer on the bottom of the prepared pan.

3. Arrange the apricots cut side down over the bottom of the pan, keeping them as evenly spaced as possible. (This will become the top of the cake, so you want things looking cute when you turn it out.) Set aside.

4. Preheat the oven to 350°F.

5. **Make the cake:** In a high-speed blender, combine the granulated sugar and cardamom seeds and blend until fragrant and well combined, about 1 minute. Set aside.

6. In a medium bowl, whisk together the flour, baking powder, salt, and baking soda. Set aside.

7. In a large bowl, whisk together the cardamom sugar,

recipe continues

olive oil, yogurt, eggs, and vanilla.

8. Add about one-third of the dry ingredients to the wet ingredients and stir to combine. Add about one-third of the milk and stir again. Continue alternating until all the dry ingredients and milk have been added.

9. Spread the batter in an even layer over the apricots and topping and bake for 45 to 55 minutes, until the cake is golden brown and a toothpick inserted in the center comes out clean.

10. Allow the cake to cool on a cooling rack for 5 minutes. Place a serving platter over the top and very carefully flip to invert the cake, leaving it in the pan. Wait about 1 minute before lifting the pan. If any of the apricots have stuck, just place them back on the cake.

11. To serve: In a small bowl, whisk together the honey with 1 tablespoon of warm water. Brush the glaze over the cake and serve warm or at room temperature with dollops of yogurt.

12. Store leftovers in an airtight container at room temperature for up to 2 days.

wow
salads

In the ten years that I've been developing and sharing recipes, I've realized that there's one thing that people are always losing their minds over: salads. As in, sophisticated-but-effortless, **layered-yet-simple** dishes that can be a side, a main, or even a condiment of sorts when heaped on top of something else. I totally get it—a meal is instantly more delicious when you layer up different **flavors and textures**, and a great salad is exactly that. This chapter is **your essential salad lineup**, an assortment of recipes that each add their own "wow" factor to a spread, whether it's a spice-infused vinaigrette, a bold combination of citrus, or big chunks of olive oil-y bread. And yet none of them require a lot of time, or even a fork.

tomato and bread salad with olives, oregano, and sage

Serves 4 to 6

FOR THE SALAD

½ loaf sourdough, torn into 1- to 1½-inch chunks (8 cups total)

⅓ cup extra-virgin olive oil

1½ teaspoons flaky sea salt, plus more for serving

6 medium tomatoes, chopped into bite-size chunks (I love heirloom for this)

½ small red onion, sliced into thin half-moons

½ cup black olives, such as dry cured (my favorite for this dish) or Kalamata

1 cup large-chunk crumbles of sheep's milk feta

⅓ cup torn fresh oregano leaves, plus more for garnish

Freshly ground black pepper to taste

FOR THE DRESSING

¼ cup red wine vinegar

2 teaspoons honey

1 medium garlic clove, grated

¾ teaspoon kosher salt, plus more to taste

Freshly ground black pepper to taste

¾ cup extra-virgin olive oil

I'm not going to overcomplicate this—we're making panzanella here. But not the kind of cute little bread salad that you pick at with a fork. No, I want full-on salad savagery—big chunks of bread for hand swabbing through the dressing, wedges of tomato juicing their sweetness over the buttery olives and salty hunks of feta, and earthy sage and oregano taking this dish to more of a sea-breezy place. If it's all dribbling down your chin between sips of crisp white wine, you are doing it completely right.

1. Preheat the oven to 425°F.

2. Start the salad: Arrange the bread on a baking sheet in a single layer, drizzle with the olive oil, and sprinkle with the flaky salt. Toast for about 15 minutes, until lightly golden. Set aside to cool slightly.

3. While the bread toasts, make the dressing: In a medium bowl, whisk together the vinegar, honey, garlic, salt, and a couple cracks of pepper. While whisking, slowly stream in the olive oil until fully incorporated. Season with more salt and pepper, if needed, and set aside.

4. Finish the salad: Place the toasted bread in a serving bowl with the tomatoes, onion, olives, and feta. Sprinkle with the oregano and drizzle with the dressing. Gently toss to combine and finish with a few cracks of pepper and a good pinch of flaky salt. Let the salad sit for at least 10 minutes for all the flavors to meld before serving.

smashed cucumber salad with sumac and sesame

Serves 4

12 small Persian cucumbers

½ teaspoon kosher salt, plus more to taste

¼ cup sesame seeds, toasted in a dry pan until fragrant

2 tablespoons extra-virgin olive oil

Juice of ½ lemon

1½ tablespoons pomegranate molasses (see page 24)

2 teaspoons honey

1 medium garlic clove, grated

1 teaspoon grated fresh ginger

1 teaspoon ground sumac

½ to 1 teaspoon Aleppo pepper or red chile flakes (depending on how much heat you're into)

Whenever I go out for Chinese or Japanese food, one of my favorite parts of the meal is the little salads and pickled condiments that come out before everything else. (Very on-brand for me.) The one I always reach for first is the smashed cucumbers, which are usually bathed in sesame oil, vinegar, garlic, ginger, and chiles. I realized it's a dish that I could easily pull together with the pantry staples I usually have on hand, so I swapped out the vinegar for tart pomegranate molasses, added olive oil (obviously), and sprinkled it with Aleppo pepper and sesame seeds. The result is a great sidecar salad that's just as refreshing, cool, and balanced as the original but with a fun twist.

1. Using the side of a large knife, give the cucumbers a smash. Cut or tear the cukes into medium chunks (about 1 inch).

2. In a medium bowl, season the cucumber chunks with the salt. Let them sit for 10 minutes.

3. Meanwhile, in a large bowl, whisk together the sesame seeds, olive oil, lemon juice, pomegranate molasses, honey, garlic, ginger, sumac, and Aleppo.

4. Drain off any liquid from the cucumbers, add them to the bowl, and toss to coat. Season with more salt, if needed.

halloumi-dusted grilled veg salad with toasted spice vinaigrette

Serves 2 to 4

FOR THE GRILLED VEGETABLES

1 medium eggplant

2 medium zucchini

Kosher salt and freshly ground black pepper to taste

¼ cup extra virgin olive oil

FOR THE TOASTED SPICE VINAIGRETTE

3 tablespoons extra-virgin olive oil

2 tablespoons red wine vinegar

Grated zest and juice of ½ lemon

2 teaspoons honey

1 medium garlic clove, minced

1 teaspoon cumin seeds, toasted in a dry pan until fragrant and then ground (I like using a mortar and pestle)

1 teaspoon fennel seeds

½ teaspoon kosher salt

Freshly ground black pepper to taste

FOR ASSEMBLY

3 medium heirloom tomatoes (about 1 pound), cut into ¼-inch-thick slices

Flaky sea salt

⅓ cup pine nuts, toasted in a dry pan until fragrant

⅓ cup grated Halloumi (use the largest holes on a box grater)

Handful of fresh basil leaves

Grilling veg is the ultimate life hack—just throw things on there for a handful of minutes, and you don't need more than a great sauce or vinaigrette for a complete and delicious dish. Grilled veg like eggplant and zucchini are real standouts because they get tender and charred in very little time and soak up this cumin- and fennel-infused vinaigrette like little sponges. Then I finish things off with an almost obnoxiously liberal sprinkling of grated salty Halloumi.

1. Make the grilled vegetables: Peel the eggplant and zucchini vertically, leaving small strips of skin behind (purely for aesthetics; we love it). Slice the eggplant and zucchini into ½-inch-thick pieces and arrange them on a baking sheet. Sprinkle everything with salt and let sit for 5 minutes. Pat dry with a towel.

2. While the vegetables sit, make the vinaigrette: In a medium bowl, whisk together the olive oil, vinegar, lemon zest and juice, honey, garlic, cumin, fennel, salt, and a couple cracks of pepper. Set aside.

3. Finish the grilled veg: Preheat the grill or grill pan to high heat. (see Note)

4. On the baking sheet, drizzle the eggplant and zucchini with the olive oil and season with about ½ teaspoon of salt and a few cracks of pepper, using your hands to make sure they're well coated. Grill the vegetables until golden, about 5 minutes. Flip and repeat on the other side, about another 5 minutes.

5. Assemble the salad: Lay the grilled vegetables on a serving platter. Add the tomatoes, season with a pinch of flaky salt, and top with the dressing, pine nuts, Halloumi, and basil and serve.

Note: If you don't have access to a grill, you could get a nice sear on the veg in a pan on the stove. Heat 2 tablespoons of olive oil in a large skillet over medium heat. When the oil shimmers, add the veggies (seasoned all over with salt and pepper) in batches so you don't crowd the pan. Sear until everything has a nice char all over, about 8 minutes for the eggplant and 10 minutes for the zucchini.

sugar snap almond crunch salad with herbed avocado cream

Serves 4

FOR THE AVOCADO CREAM

1 cup full-fat Greek yogurt

½ medium avocado

⅓ cup fresh basil leaves

¼ cup chopped fresh chives

¼ cup fresh mint leaves

¼ cup fresh flat-leaf parsley leaves

Juice of ½ lemon

1 medium garlic clove

½ teaspoon kosher salt

FOR THE SALAD

2 (8-ounce) bags sugar snap peas (4 cups), thinly sliced lengthwise (no need to be perfect!)

Handful of fresh mint leaves

Handful of fresh basil leaves

Handful of fresh flat-leaf parsley leaves

½ cup blanched sliced almonds, lightly toasted in a dry pan until fragrant

5 tablespoons extra-virgin olive oil

Grated zest and juice of 1 lemon

1 teaspoon kosher salt

I love a light, bright, crunchy salad moment, and this is *the* moment. It's a dish that captures that special time when fresh green produce is just popping up at the market in the spring and you don't want anything to get in the way of its delicately sweet flavor. Instead of getting tossed in with a bunch of greens, the sugar snap peas are truly the star, and by julienning them (which may take some patience, but I promise you it's worth it!), they perfectly cradle the simple vinaigrette and flecks of fresh herbs, while still showing off their signature texture. Heap this on top of a rich avocado cream, grab two forks, and eat it straight out of the bowl with your person.

1. **Make the avocado cream:** In a high-speed blender, combine the yogurt, avocado, basil, chives, mint, parsley, lemon juice, garlic, and salt. Blend until smooth and a gorgeous green color. Set aside or store in a sealed container in the fridge for up to 24 hours.

2. **Make the salad:** In a large bowl, combine the sugar snap peas with the mint, basil, and parsley. Add all but a couple tablespoons of the almonds plus the olive oil, lemon zest and juice, and salt and toss to combine.

3. Spread the avocado cream over a serving platter and lay the salad over the top. Sprinkle with the reserved almonds and serve.

herb and celery leaf salad with hazelnuts, cherries, and long-hots

Serves 2 to 4

⅓ cup hazelnuts

Leaves from 1 bunch fresh parsley

Leaves from 1 bunch fresh mint

Leaves from 1 bunch fresh cilantro

1½ cups thinly sliced celery (about 5 stalks), leaves included

1½ cups fresh cherries, pitted and halved (see Note)

½ medium long-hot chile, stemmed and thinly sliced (seeded for less heat, or omitted altogether)

¼ cup extra-virgin olive oil

Juice of 1 lemon

1 teaspoon flaky sea salt

Note: You can sub an equal amount of pomegranate seeds for the cherries for that same tart-sweet burst of flavor. Other great options are dried fruits like currants, sour cherries, and chopped apricots.

Herb salads are all over Israel. It's not uncommon to get a bowl of fresh herbs tossed with olive oil, lemon juice, and salt and *that's it*. It taught me that parsley, mint, and cilantro are so much more than garnishes and can be used just as you would lettuce. Then one day, I had the famous "lali" salad at one of my favorite restaurants in Tel Aviv, HaBasta. It was a bowl of cilantro, chiles, and cherries. Nothing else, end of story. The combination stopped me in my tracks—it was so nuanced with the layers of grassy herbaceousness, green heat, and sweet-tartness and yet so unbelievably simple. I wanted to preserve that simplicity while also sneaking in a little more variety in terms of flavor, texture, and heat. The result is a dish that's unlike most of the salads you've had before, and yet once you try it, you'll wonder why you haven't been making fruity, nutty herb salads your entire life.

1. In a small skillet, toast the hazelnuts over medium heat until toasted and fragrant, about 10 minutes. Rub them in a dry towel to remove their skins, then give them a rough chop.

2. In a large salad bowl, combine the toasted hazelnuts with the parsley, mint, cilantro, celery, cherries, and chile (if using). Give everything a toss to combine and finish with the olive oil, lemon juice, and flaky salt. Toss and serve.

creamy feta wedge salad with garlicky bread crumbs and mint

Serves 4 to 6

FOR THE DRESSING

1 cup large-chunk crumbles of sheep's milk feta

⅓ cup full-fat Greek yogurt

¼ cup mayonnaise

3 tablespoons extra-virgin olive oil

1 medium garlic clove, peeled

Freshly ground black pepper to taste

FOR THE GARLICKY BREAD CRUMBS

¼ cup extra-virgin olive oil

1 small garlic clove, grated

¾ cup panko bread crumbs

½ teaspoon kosher salt

FOR THE SALAD

1 head iceberg lettuce

3 Persian or mini cucumbers, cut into ½-inch-thick half-moons

1 cup cherry tomatoes, halved

⅓ cup chopped fresh chives

Large handful of fresh mint

Extra-virgin olive oil, for drizzling

Freshly ground black pepper to taste

This dish is the ultimate mash-up between two gold-standard salads: the classic steakhouse wedge (think iceberg lettuce and way too much creamy dressing) and the feta-flecked, veggie-stuffed chopped salad I grew up eating. I definitely surprised myself a little bit when I reached for iceberg lettuce as the base, but once I loaded it up with cherry tomatoes and cukes, fresh mint, and garlicky bread crumbs that work their way into every crevice and cranny, I realized it was the only choice. But the real star is the rich, creamy feta and yogurt dressing. I highly recommend serving some on the side for extra dunking, in addition to keeping a batch in your fridge for an impromptu salad or dip moment.

1. Make the dressing: In a high-speed blender, combine the feta, yogurt, mayo, olive oil, garlic, and a few cracks of pepper. Blend until smooth and set aside.

2. Make the bread crumbs: Heat the olive oil in a small pan over medium heat. When the oil shimmers, add the garlic. Cook just until the garlic begins to lightly brown, less than 1 minute, and add the panko. Season with the salt, toss to coat in the oil, and cook until golden brown and fragrant, about 2 minutes. Set aside.

3. Make the salad: Cut the iceberg lettuce in half and remove the tough core. Halve each half and then cut each quarter in half to make eight wedges.

4. Place the lettuce in a large salad bowl and scatter with the cucumbers and tomatoes. Drizzle with the dressing and sprinkle with the bread crumbs. Finish with the chives and mint plus a drizzle of olive oil and a few cracks of pepper.

wow salads

crispy spiced chickpea "crunch salad" with pomegranate seeds

Serves 6

I love a crispy chickpea, but I didn't want to give you a recipe for them until I could be 100 percent sure that my recipe would get you the perfectly crunchy, spiced results you deserve. Well, now we're here, and I've done you right. It's not too difficult to achieve using canned chickpeas (bless them), but you do have to make sure they're drained and dried very well. From there, it's just a matter of slathering them in a sultry paprika and Aleppo mixture, roasting them, and sprinkling those crisp little bad boys all over a bed of carrots, radishes, and cukes, which are the crunchy trifecta of the veg world. With a tangy sumac and pomegranate molasses vinaigrette and sweet-tart pomegranate seeds, this dish is designed to be your new go-to everyday salad.

FOR THE CRISPY CHICKPEAS

1 (15-ounce) can chickpeas, drained, rinsed, and dried well

2 tablespoons extra-virgin olive oil

2 teaspoons paprika

1 teaspoon ground cumin

½ teaspoon kosher salt

¼ teaspoon Aleppo pepper or red chile flakes

FOR THE DRESSING

½ cup extra virgin olive oil

1 medium shallot, minced

2 tablespoons pomegranate molasses (see page 24)

1 tablespoon red wine vinegar

1 teaspoon ground sumac

1 teaspoon kosher salt

½ teaspoon freshly ground black pepper

FOR THE SALAD

2 large carrots (orange or rainbow), sliced into thin coins

1 large Persian cucumber, sliced into thin rounds

5 radishes, thinly sliced

½ medium red onion, thinly sliced

1. Preheat the oven to 425°F.

2. Make the crispy chickpeas: In a medium bowl, toss the chickpeas with the olive oil, paprika, cumin, salt, and Aleppo. Spread the chickpeas in a single layer on a baking sheet and roast for 25 to 30 minutes, until they are golden and very crispy. Set aside to cool.

3. While the chickpeas crisp, make the dressing: In a medium bowl, whisk together the olive oil, shallot, pomegranate molasses, vinegar, sumac, salt, and pepper. Adjust the seasoning with more salt, if needed.

4. Make the salad: In a serving bowl, combine about three-quarters of the crispy chickpeas with the carrots, cucumber, radishes, onion, and pomegranate seeds. Add about three-quarters of the parsley, dill, and mint and toss to combine.

1 cup pomegranate seeds

½ cup fresh flat-leaf parsley leaves, roughly chopped

½ cup fresh dill, roughly chopped

½ cup fresh mint leaves, roughly chopped

5. Drizzle with the dressing and finish with the remaining herbs and crispy chickpeas.

loaded herbed potato salad with labaneh and preserved lemons

Serves 4 to 6

2 pounds new potatoes

½ teaspoon kosher salt, plus more as needed

½ cup Labaneh (page 42)

2 tablespoons fresh lemon juice (about ½ lemon), plus more to taste

¼ cup finely chopped fresh flat-leaf parsley leaves

⅓ cup packed finely chopped fresh dill, plus more for serving

¼ cup finely chopped fresh mint, plus more for serving

3 tablespoons extra-virgin olive oil, plus more for serving

2 medium garlic cloves, minced

2 tablespoons rinsed and finely chopped rind of Preserved Lemons (page 67)

1 teaspoon champagne or white wine vinegar

½ teaspoon ground cumin

Freshly ground black pepper to taste

1 large shallot, thinly sliced into rings

I don't think you can have a chapter of salad recipes and *not* include a potato salad. For me it will always be the OG, the one salad you find on just about any summer party spread, and the one that no matter whether you're team mustard or mayo will always be comforting, satisfying, and filling. That said, I do think it's time for a little freshening up, so I looked to a few of my pantry favorites to get the job done. Tangy, creamy labaneh and bright preserved lemons are perfect for cutting through the rich starchiness of buttery new potatoes, and a drizzle of cumin-scented vinaigrette with heaps of fresh herbs keeps things feeling current. It's still the ideal picnic or potluck dish, and it's great made the day before.

1. Place the potatoes in a large pot and add enough cold water to cover by 1 inch. Add a generous handful of salt and bring to a boil over medium-high heat. Reduce to a simmer and cook until the potatoes are fork-tender, 15 to 20 minutes. Drain and set aside to cool slightly.

2. While the potatoes cook, make the dressing: In a medium bowl, combine the labaneh, lemon juice, parsley, dill, mint, olive oil, garlic, preserved lemon, vinegar, cumin, salt, and a few cracks of pepper. Whisk until completely smooth.

3. Slice the potatoes in half, or quarters if on the larger side, and transfer them to a serving bowl with the shallot. Toss with the dressing and season with more salt, pepper, and/or lemon juice, if needed.

4. Finish with more dill and mint, a drizzle of olive oil, and a couple cracks of pepper.

plum and baby gem salad with burrata, pickled shallots, and dukkah

Serves 4

FOR THE QUICK-PICKLED SHALLOTS

3 small shallots, sliced into thin rings

½ cup apple cider vinegar

1 tablespoon honey

1 teaspoon kosher salt

½ teaspoon whole black peppercorns

FOR THE VINAIGRETTE

1 tablespoon red wine vinegar

1 tablespoon Dijon mustard

1 teaspoon honey

1 teaspoon grated orange zest

¼ cup extra-virgin olive oil

Kosher salt and freshly ground black pepper to taste

FOR THE SALAD

2 heads baby gem lettuce, leaves separated

2 ripe plums, pitted and sliced

1 (4-ounce) ball burrata

¼ cup Fennel Seed Pistachio Dukkah (page 92)

Fresh mint leaves, for garnish

Extra-virgin olive oil, for serving

Flaky sea salt, for serving

You might think this salad is all about the burrata, the oozy dream cheese, but I majorly beg to differ—it's the plums that are giving main-character energy. I wanted to come up with a fresh, easy salad that played up their tart sweetness instead of trying to tame it. You could easily substitute persimmon, which I can never get enough of, especially because they're a little harder to come by in North America. In the fall, when you start to see them in the grocery store, be sure to snap up some fuyus (firm but with a little give) and try them here too. Citrus and pomegranate would also be delish.

1. **Make the pickled shallots:** Add the shallots to a 16-ounce glass jar and set aside.

2. In a small pot, combine the apple cider vinegar, honey, salt, and peppercorns with ½ cup of water. Bring to a simmer over medium heat and simmer until the honey has dissolved, about 5 minutes. Pour the brine over the shallots and allow to sit for 30 minutes before using (see Note).

3. **Make the vinaigrette:** In a medium bowl, whisk together the red wine vinegar, mustard, honey, and orange zest. While

whisking, slowly stream in the olive oil until well combined. Season with salt and pepper and whisk again. Set aside.

4. **Make the salad:** Arrange the baby gem leaves on a large platter. Lay the plum slices over the top, tear the burrata into bite-size chunks, and scatter them over the plums. Drizzle the salad with the dressing, then sprinkle on the shallots, dukkah, and mint.

5. Finish with one last slick of olive oil and pinch of flaky salt and serve.

Note: The pickled shallots will last in the fridge for up to 1 week, if you want to make them ahead.

halloumi, citrus, and fennel salad with aleppo honey and mint

Serves 4

4 tablespoons extra-virgin olive oil

1 teaspoon fennel seeds

1 (8-ounce) package Halloumi, cut into 1-inch-thick slabs

4 assorted citrus fruits, such as grapefruit, Cara Cara oranges, or blood oranges

2 tablespoons honey

½ teaspoon Aleppo pepper

1 small fennel bulb, trimmed and very thinly sliced, fronds reserved for garnish (if you have them)

1 large lemon, halved

¼ cup roasted, salted pistachios, chopped

Flaky sea salt, for serving

¼ cup fresh mint leaves

With all due respect to my other great love, celery, fennel will always be on repeat in my raw salad rotaysh because I love its subtle anisey flavor and not-too-watery crunch. Plus, it never gets mushy or sad when left to marinate in a vinaigrette. So I immediately thought of it when assembling this citrus-forward salad that needed a hit of texture and something fresh and herbaceous to balance out the tart punch. To bring it all together and make it feel like a really special moment on the table, I added salty, meaty slabs of Halloumi drizzled with Aleppo-infused honey. There's not a spot on your taste buds that this year-round salad doesn't hit.

1. Heat 2 tablespoons of the olive oil and the fennel seeds in a large skillet over medium heat until the fennel is fragrant, 1 to 2 minutes. Add the Halloumi to the pan and sear until deeply browned, about 2 minutes on each side. Remove the pan from the heat and transfer the Halloumi to a plate and set aside.

2. Slice off the very top and bottom from each piece of citrus. Carefully run your knife around the fruit to remove the peel and white pith. Cut the fruit into ¼-inch-thick slices, discarding any seeds.

3. In a small bowl, whisk together the honey and Aleppo.

4. Arrange alternating slices of the citrus, fennel bulb, and Halloumi on a serving platter. Drizzle with the remaining 2 tablespoons olive oil and squeeze the lemon on top.

5. Finish with a ribbon of the Aleppo honey—feel free to reserve some for serving on the side. Sprinkle with the pistachios and flaky salt, and tuft with the fennel fronds, if you have them, and the mint. Serve immediately.

CHAPTER 5

hot new
side
piece

These are your **sidecars**, your **meal enhancers**, your **main-dish ride-or-dies**. These recipes are all thoughtful plates of veg that will complement any savory preparation in this book, or whatever else you happen to be cooking. And if preparing veg-forward meals is relatively new to you, this is a great place to start because we're keeping things super stripped down and simple, **letting the veg and their natural flavors shine through** with just the right assist from simple seasonings and condiments. You could also easily turn any of these dishes into mains by adding a grain, legume, dip, salad, and/or fresh bread. Or whip up a few of them for a light but satisfying spread. Because each of these recipes pulls from the same Middle Eastern inspo, they can be **mixed and matched seamlessly**.

black lime–seared radishes with crispy capers

Serves 4

2 tablespoons unsalted butter

2 tablespoons extra-virgin olive oil

1½ teaspoons black lime powder (see Note)

2 large bunches Easter or French breakfast radishes with leaves attached, rinsed and dried well

¼ cup brined capers, drained and dried

½ teaspoon kosher salt

Freshly ground black pepper to taste

¼ cup chopped fresh flat-leaf parsley leaves

¼ cup chopped fresh cilantro leaves

2 tablespoons chopped fresh mint leaves

Juice of ½ lime

1 tablespoon sesame seeds, toasted in a dry pan until fragrant

Flaky sea salt, for serving

Laffa (page 236) or Jerusalem Bagel Dinner Rolls (page 232), for serving

Garlicky Tahini (page 59) or Labaneh (page 42), for serving (optional)

There's something about the lush bundles of candy-colored radishes at the market that's irresistible to me. Part of it has to do with my fantasy of lounging in a Paris park while eating them spicy and raw with good salty butter, but part of it is because I love how succulent, mild, and meaty they get when cooked. It opens up a whole new way of enjoying them, which I like to complement with the bright, sour-salty notes of black lime and capers. When served as a side, these radishes are the perfect way to add brightness and substance to another dish. Or you can enjoy these on their own with good bread like laffa or Jerusalem bagel dinner rolls and a drizzle of tahini or labaneh.

1. In a large skillet, combine the butter, olive oil, and black lime powder over medium-low heat. When the butter melts, increase the heat to medium and add the radishes and capers. Season with the salt and a few cracks of pepper and sear, stirring occasionally, until the radishes are bright and slightly blistered but still crisp, 2 to 4 minutes. Remove the pan from the heat and allow the radishes to cool slightly.

2. Scatter over the parsley, cilantro, mint, lime juice, and sesame seeds and toss to combine. Transfer everything to a serving plate and finish with flaky salt. Serve with laffa or rolls and a drizzle of tahini or labaneh, if desired.

Note: Black limes, also known as Persian or sun-dried limes, are often used in Middle Eastern and North African cooking for a layer of sour, salty flavor. To add them to a dish is to add a similar lift and brightness as fresh citrus but with even more earthy depth and complexity. You can easily find them in international markets, and you can use a Microplane to grate the rind anywhere black lime is called for in these recipes. Or you could grind them in a spice grinder and store the extra ground lime in a sealed container in your spice drawer.

za'atar asparagus with walnut-date freekeh and tahini vinaigrette

FOR THE ZA'ATAR ASPARAGUS

2 tablespoons extra-virgin olive oil

2 teaspoons Za'atar (page 25), plus more for serving

1 teaspoon kosher salt

1 bunch asparagus, tough ends trimmed and cut into 1-inch pieces on the bias

FOR THE TAHINI VINAIGRETTE

¼ cup tahini

Juice of ½ lemon

1½ teaspoons red wine vinegar

1½ teaspoons honey

½ medium garlic clove, grated

½ teaspoon kosher salt

Freshly ground black pepper to taste

FOR ASSEMBLY

2 cups cooked freekeh (see Note)

⅓ cup raw walnuts, lightly toasted in a dry pan until fragrant and crushed

3 Medjool dates, pitted and finely chopped

1 tablespoon rinsed and finely chopped rind of Preserved Lemons (page 67)

I wanted to show the sultry, moody side of asparagus, which we normally think of as bright, fresh, and perky—just like its spring veg siblings. But when you season asparagus with earthy za'atar and roast it until it's almost charred, it officially enters its emo era. I keep things from going too far to the dark side by layering the asparagus over a freekeh salad flecked with nuts, dates, and preserved lemons and drizzled with a creamy tahini vinaigrette. When topped with a jammy egg, it becomes the ideal breakfast or lunch. The tahini vinaigrette is also a rockstar on its own, whether you're drizzling it over a simple salad or roasted veg dishes.

Note: If you like to meal prep, I highly recommend prepping the freekeh, jammy eggs, and vinaigrette ahead of time and storing them separately in the fridge for up to 5 days, which means you can throw this dish together in minutes. You could sub bulgur, quinoa, or wild rice for the freekeh.

1. Preheat the oven to 450°F.

2. Make the asparagus: In a small bowl, stir together the olive oil, za'atar, and salt.

3. Arrange the asparagus on a baking sheet and drizzle with the za'atar oil. Toss to coat well and roast for about 15 minutes, until lightly charred.

4. While the asparagus roasts, make the vinaigrette: In a medium bowl, combine the tahini, lemon juice, vinegar, honey, garlic, salt, a couple cracks of pepper, and ¼ cup of water. Whisk until smooth and set aside.

recipe and ingredients continue

2 tablespoons extra-virgin
olive oil

½ teaspoon kosher salt

2 large eggs, cooked to jammy
(see page 214), peeled and
halved (see Note)

Flaky sea salt to taste

Freshly ground black pepper
to taste

5. Assemble: In a large bowl,
combine the freekeh with
the walnuts, dates, preserved
lemon, olive oil, and salt. Toss
to mix well.

6. Heap the freekeh on a
serving plate and place the

roasted asparagus on top or
alongside. Top with the eggs
and drizzle everything with
the vinaigrette. Finish with
a sprinkle of flaky salt and a
couple cracks of pepper and
serve.

fennel and potato gratin with almond-date crumb

Serves 6

FOR THE GRATIN

2 tablespoons unsalted butter, plus more for greasing

1 tablespoon extra-virgin olive oil

2 medium leeks, ends trimmed, dark green leaves removed, halved vertically and rinsed then sliced into ½-inch-thick rings

1 tablespoon ground fennel seeds (see Notes, page 152)

2 teaspoons ground coriander (see Notes, page 152)

4 medium garlic cloves, finely chopped

2 teaspoons kosher salt

½ teaspoon freshly ground black pepper

4 medium Russet potatoes, peeled and thinly sliced

4 medium fennel bulbs (see Notes, page 152), ends trimmed, sliced ⅛ inch thick (I like a mandoline for this)

1½ cups heavy cream

1¼ cups freshly grated Parmesan

1 cup grated Gruyère

½ lemon

FOR THE ALMOND-DATE CRUMB

¼ cup extra-virgin olive oil

1 medium garlic clove, finely chopped

My obsession with fennel is no secret, but it sometimes gets to the point where I have to ask myself, *Does this dish really need it?* When it comes to this roasty, creamy gratin, though, the answer is most definitely YES. Sweet, tender fennel is what gives this otherwise traditional cheesy potato casserole that little something extra, which I tease out even more with fennel seeds and coriander, plus a crunchy crumb topping that gets another hit of rich sweetness from almonds and dates. It's a special-feeling dish that would be at home on a holiday table, or make it for a casual, cozy weeknight meal with a simple salad.

1. **Make the gratin:** Preheat the oven to 375°F. Grease a 9 × 13-inch baking dish with butter and set aside.

2. In a large skillet, combine the butter and olive oil over medium heat. When the butter begins to foam, add the leeks, fennel seeds, and coriander. Sauté, stirring occasionally, until the leeks have just softened, about 2 minutes. Add the garlic, 1 teaspoon of the salt, and ¼ teaspoon of the pepper. Sauté until the garlic is fragrant and the leeks have softened completely, another 2 to 3 minutes. Remove the

pan from the heat and allow the mixture to cool slightly.

3. In a large bowl, combine the potatoes, fennel bulbs, cream, 1 cup of the Parm, ¾ cup of the Gruyère, the remaining 1 teaspoon salt, remaining ¼ teaspoon pepper, and the leek mixture. Mix well.

4. Transfer the mixture to the prepared baking dish. Sprinkle with the remaining ¼ cup Parm and ¼ cup Gruyère and cover with foil. Bake for 45 minutes to 1 hour, until the vegetables are tender.

recipe and ingredients continue

hot new side piece

1 cup panko bread crumbs

1 teaspoon flaky sea salt,
plus more to taste

¼ cup almonds, toasted in a dry
pan until fragrant and chopped

⅓ cup pitted and chopped
Medjool dates (4 to 5 dates)

Grated zest of ½ lemon

Notes: I recommend placing
coriander and fennel seeds
in a mortar and pestle and
crushing them before using.

You could swap in a
small bulb of peeled and
thinly sliced celeriac for the
fennel, or use it in addition
to the fennel and reduce the
amount of potato you use by
a roughly equal measure. It
has a similar earthy sweetness
to fennel, and the two get
along really nicely.

5. Remove the foil and bake for
another 25 to 30 minutes, until
the top is bubbling and golden.

**6. While the gratin bakes, make
the crumb:** Heat the olive oil in
a medium pot or skillet over
medium heat. When the oil
shimmers, add the garlic and
sauté until just fragrant, about
20 seconds. (You don't want it
to brown.) Add the panko and
flaky salt and toss to coat in
the oil.

7. Reduce the heat to medium-
low and toast the panko,
stirring occasionally, until nice
and golden, about 3 minutes.
Remove the pan from the heat
and allow the mixture to cool
slightly.

8. In a medium bowl, combine
the toasted panko with the
almonds, dates, and lemon
zest. Season with more flaky
salt, if desired.

9. To assemble the gratin,
squeeze the lemon over the
top, cover the gratin with an
even layer of the crumb, and
serve.

charred brussels with pomegranate butter

Serves 4

FOR THE BRUSSELS

2 pounds Brussels sprouts

2 tablespoons extra-virgin olive oil

1 teaspoon kosher salt, plus more to taste

FOR THE POMEGRANATE BUTTER

2 tablespoons salted butter

1 tablespoon extra-virgin olive oil

2 tablespoons pomegranate molasses (see page 24)

2 medium garlic cloves, finely chopped

1 tablespoon Aleppo pepper or red chile flakes (optional)

FOR SERVING

⅓ cup pomegranate seeds

2 tablespoons chopped fresh cilantro leaves

Hear me out: I know that Brussels can be . . . controversial; I mean, even I struggled with them well into my twenties. Seriously, every time I saw them on a plate I'd be like *why???* But the root of all that drama is poorly cooked (usually overcooked) sprouts. When you roast them up until they're richly caramelized, then shellac them in pomegranate molasses–spiked butter, the whole situation is much more agreeable. And by agreeable, I mean completely irresistible. Zero traces of bitterness or funk, only crispy bites you'll pop until you can't stop.

1. Preheat the oven to 425°F. Place a baking sheet on the middle rack to preheat while the oven heats. (This will help the sprouts crisp up.)

2. Make the Brussels: Trim and discard the stem ends of the Brussels and then slice them in half. In a large bowl, toss them with the olive oil and salt. Carefully transfer the Brussels to the hot baking sheet and arrange them cut side down.

3. Roast for 15 to 20 minutes, until the Brussels sprouts are golden.

4. While they roast, make the pomegranate butter: Heat the butter and olive oil in a small skillet over medium heat. When the butter begins to brown a little, add the pomegranate molasses, garlic, and Aleppo (if using). Swirl to combine and cook just until the garlic softens and is fragrant, about 1 minute.

5. To serve: Drizzle the pomegranate butter over the roasted Brussels sprouts and toss to coat well. Transfer the Brussels to a serving plate and finish with the pomegranate seeds, cilantro, and more salt to taste.

hot new side piece

crispy, crunchy potato chunks with preserved lemon toum and golden amba pepper sauce

Serves 4

2 pounds Yukon Gold potatoes (around 6), peeled, halved, then cut into thirds

1 teaspoon kosher salt, plus more as needed

⅓ cup extra-virgin olive oil

Freshly ground black pepper to taste

Preserved Lemon Toum (page 41), for serving

Golden Amba Pepper Sauce (page 34), for serving (see Note)

Note: I love the combination of garlicky toum with the amba pepper sauce, but go with what you have or are in the mood for—Celery Zhoug (page 30) or Fast 'n' Fresh Harissa (page 33) would also be very tasty here. Also, if my experience with these is any indication, you might want to double this recipe so you don't eat all of them before they even make it to the table.

I've never in my life met someone who doesn't love a crispy, crunchy potato, so I felt like that deserved a sexy moment in this book. And the only way you can serve snappy-on-the-outside, fluffy-on-the-inside potatoes, in my opinion, is slathered with an insanely garlicky and creamy sauce, aka toum. To balance it out, we're also drizzling them with amba pepper sauce, which not only looks like sunshine on a plate but tastes like it too. Don't worry about these getting cold; everyone will be devouring them straight off the baking sheet like the crispy tater nachos they are.

1. Preheat the oven to 450°F. Place a baking sheet in the oven to heat while the oven heats.

2. Place the potatoes in a large pot and add enough cold water to cover by 1 inch. Add a generous pinch of salt and bring to a boil over medium-high heat. Boil until a knife slides through the potatoes, about 20 minutes. Drain the potatoes in a colander and give them a good shake, which will help give them a fluffy texture that will eventually become a nice, crispy shell.

3. Return the potatoes to the pot, drizzle with the olive oil, and add 1 teaspoon salt and a couple cracks of pepper. Toss to coat. Carefully remove the preheated baking sheet from the oven and spread the potatoes on it in an even layer. Roast for 55 minutes to 1 hour, shaking the pan about halfway through, until the potatoes are golden and crispy.

4. Serve hot with your favorite sauces.

rosemary-honey halloumi fries

————————————————————————————————— **Serves 4 (makes about 2 cups fries)**

8 fresh rosemary sprigs

1 cup panko bread crumbs

Freshly ground black pepper

1 cup all-purpose flour

2 large eggs

1 (8-ounce) package Halloumi, rinsed and patted dry

1 cup refined avocado or grapeseed oil

¼ cup honey, plus more to taste, for serving

At first I wasn't sure if people would want to take the time to coat cheese in bread crumbs and fry it. But after trying it out one night, I decided that *everyone* is going to want to do it, so here we freakin' go. These are pretty much your gooey, salty, fatty, crispy, crunchy DIY mozzarella sticks, except we're using Halloumi, which holds its shape really nicely and cuts through the richness of the breading. We're also adding some rosemary to the dredge plus a drizzle of honey to finish things off to, you know, keep it classy.

1. Strip the needles from 5 of the rosemary sprigs and finely chop them.

2. On a large plate, combine the chopped rosemary with the panko and season with a few cracks of pepper. Add the flour to another large plate and season with pepper. And in a medium shallow bowl, beat the eggs and season with pepper.

3. Slice the Halloumi into ½-inch-thick fry shapes. Gently pat them dry again. In small batches, coat the Halloumi in the flour, followed by the eggs, and then the rosemary panko. Continue with the remaining pieces of Halloumi.

4. Line a baking sheet with paper towels.

5. Heat the oil in a large skillet over medium heat. When the oil shimmers, add enough fries to comfortably fit in the pan without overcrowding and fry until golden, about 2 minutes per side. Use a slotted spoon to transfer the fries to the lined baking sheet and repeat with the remaining Halloumi.

6. Remove the needles from the remaining 3 rosemary sprigs and fry just until crisp, about 30 seconds.

7. Place the fries in a shallow bowl, top with the fried rosemary needles, and drizzle with the honey. Serve hot.

hot new side piece

159

leeks with sumac, parm, and pine nuts

Serves 2 as a main or 4 as a side dish

2 tablespoons unsalted butter

2 tablespoons extra-virgin olive oil

4 medium leeks, ends trimmed, dark green leaves removed, halved vertically and rinsed

Kosher salt and freshly ground black pepper to taste

2 teaspoons ground sumac

½ teaspoon ground allspice

½ teaspoon ground cumin

Pinch of ground cinnamon

½ cup dry white wine, such as Sauvignon Blanc

⅓ cup freshly grated Parmesan

½ lemon, for serving

⅓ cup pine nuts, toasted in a dry pan

Fresh flat-leaf parsley leaves, for garnish

Every time I cook a dish where leeks are the star—which is more often than you'd expect—Ido completely freaks out all over again about just how incredible they are. Zero arguments here because I've always loved how they keep their shape and meaty texture even as they get luscious and buttery. Not your average side, these leeks soak up all this sumac- and allspice-infused oil in the pan—a combo that's inspired by Palestinian mussakhan. Then they get popped under the broiler with a hit of Parm for an extra-savory finish. But then again, average is not what we're about.

1. Heat the butter and olive oil in a large ovenproof skillet with a fitted lid over medium-high heat. When the butter starts to foam, add the leeks cut side down and season with salt and pepper. Allow the leeks to sear without moving them until they develop a deeply golden crust, about 3 minutes.

2. Flip the leeks and season them with more salt and pepper plus the sumac, allspice, cumin, and cinnamon. Allow the leeks to continue searing until just golden, about 3 minutes, then pour in the wine and ½ cup of water. Cover the pan and reduce the heat to medium. Allow the leeks to simmer until tender and almost all the liquid has reduced, 15 to 20 minutes. Every few minutes, spoon some of the pan sauce over the leeks to make sure they're really bathing in all that flavor.

3. Position an oven rack about 6 inches below the broiler and preheat the broiler to high.

4. Sprinkle the Parm over the leeks and transfer the pan to the oven. Broil until the cheese and leeks are melted and golden, about 10 seconds.

5. Finish with a squeeze of lemon juice and sprinkle with the pine nuts and parsley.

grilled romano beans with walnuts and tzatziki

Serves 4

3 pounds Romano beans or green beans (see Note)

¼ cup extra-virgin olive oil, plus more for serving

Kosher salt to taste

Grated zest and juice of ½ lemon

2 small garlic cloves, grated

¾ cup raw walnuts, lightly toasted in a dry pan until fragrant and then finely chopped

1½ cups Tzatziki (page 73)

Fresh mint leaves and dill, for serving

Flaky sea salt, for serving

Note: In the summer, when the farmers' markets are in full force, I highly recommend that you seek out Romano beans. But if you have trouble finding them, feel free to sub regular green beans. Also, you can skip the grilling and still have a completely solid dish! Just blanch the beans and call it a day.

Romano beans, or Italian flat beans, are just the supreme green bean. (Know what I mean?) They're steak-y and substantial, making them perfect for this lovely summer dish. I toss 'em on the grill for some nice char and smoke, then all that's left to do is to whip up a garlicky tzatziki and top with some rich, fatty toasted walnuts. It's a simple dish, but with its layers of flavors and textures, it's a real standout.

1. Preheat a grill or grill pan to medium-high heat.

2. In a large bowl, toss the beans with the olive oil and season well with salt. Add the beans to the grill or grill pan and lightly char all over, 1 to 2 minutes per side.

3. Transfer the beans to a large bowl (you can use the same one you used to toss the beans in oil) and toss them with the lemon zest and juice and garlic. Add the walnuts and toss gently to combine.

4. Arrange the beans and walnuts on a plate and dollop all over with the tzatziki. Finish with the mint, dill, a drizzle of olive oil, and a sprinkle of flaky salt.

crispy artichokes with crème fraîche and zhoug

4 lemons

4 large globe artichokes

5 cardamom pods

1¾ teaspoons kosher salt

1 teaspoon coriander seeds

½ cup extra-virgin olive oil

Flaky sea salt, for serving

1½ cups crème fraîche or Labaneh (page 42)

½ cup Celery Zhoug (page 30)

When I was growing up, a dinner that included artichokes always felt so celebratory, since I knew I would be hanging with my family around the table, picking the leaves and chatting for hours (in between the dance parties and comedy skits my sisters and I would put on for our parents). So I had to include a recipe for artichokes, especially since I know there is a mental block for a lot of people when it comes to them. Yes, as far as vegetables go, artichokes are a little high-maintenance, but no step here is overly complicated, and it takes barely any effort to end up with a gorgeous plate that would work as a starter, snack, or side.

1. Fill a large bowl with water and add the juice of one of the lemons. Set aside.

2. Use a serrated knife to remove all but 2 inches of each artichoke stalk. Then run the knife around the base of the outermost layer of leaves and break them off. Trim off the top ½ inch of each artichoke, then slice in half lengthwise and use a small spoon to scoop out the fuzzy choke and discard.

3. Rinse the cleaned artichoke under running water and immediately place it in the lemon water to prevent it from turning brown while you clean the remaining artichokes.

4. Add the cleaned artichokes to a large pot with 2 cups of water, the peel and juice of one of the lemons, the cardamom pods, 1 teaspoon of the salt, and the coriander. Cover the pot and bring to a boil over medium-high heat. Reduce the heat to medium-low and allow the artichokes to steam until a knife easily slides in, about 10 minutes.

5. Remove the artichokes from the pot and drain the cooking liquid through a fine-mesh sieve. Reserve the spices and

lemon peel and carefully pat them dry. Remove the cardamom seeds from the pods.

Heat the olive oil in a large nonstick skillet over medium-high heat. When the oil shimmers, add the reserved peel and spices, including the cardamom seeds. Add the artichokes, season with the remaining ¾ teaspoon salt, and fry until golden all over, about 6 minutes.

Sprinkle the artichokes with flaky salt and serve with the crème fraîche, zhoug, and remaining 2 lemons sliced into wedges.

Note: If you want to make the original version of this dish, just swap out the gremolata for Fennel Seed Pistachio Dukkah (page 92).

harissa honey carrots with carrot top gremolata and labaneh

FOR THE HARISSA HONEY CARROTS

¼ cup extra-virgin olive oil

3 tablespoons honey

3 tablespoons Fast 'n' Fresh Harissa (page 33)

¾ teaspoon kosher salt

½ teaspoon ground cumin

Freshly ground black pepper to taste

2 pounds small carrots, or large carrots halved lengthwise

FOR THE CARROT TOP GREMOLATA (see Note)

½ cup extra-virgin olive oil

⅓ cup shelled pistachios, toasted in a dry pan until lightly browned and then chopped

⅓ cup finely chopped carrot tops

¼ cup finely chopped fresh cilantro leaves

1 small garlic clove, grated

Grated zest of 1 lemon

½ teaspoon kosher salt

FOR ASSEMBLY

2 cups Labaneh (page 42)

Flaky sea salt

Extra-virgin olive oil

Fresh cilantro leaves

Carrots braised and glazed with honey and harissa until they were charred, sticky, and spicy sweet was one of the most popular dishes on the menu at my New York City restaurant, Dez. In its honor, I wanted to come up with a reboot, which was surprisingly difficult because it's hard to improve upon perfection. I finally figured out that by adding an herbaceous green gremolata using the carrot tops—because we love whole-vegetable, no-waste cooking—I could take this already incredible dish to the next level. When these are served over a schmear of tangy labaneh you could get lost in all those layers of flavor. I mean, just look at its centerfold moment on page 142. I pretty much guarantee you'll never make carrots any other way.

1. Preheat the oven to 450°F.

2. Make the carrots: In a small bowl, mix together the olive oil, honey, harissa, salt, cumin, and a couple cracks of black pepper. Reserve 3 tablespoons of the mixture and set aside.

3. Arrange the carrots on a baking sheet and drizzle with the honey harissa mixture. Toss to coat well and roast for 15 to 20 minutes, until golden and slightly burnt on the edges.

4. While the carrots roast, make the gremolata: In a medium bowl, mix together the olive oil, pistachios, carrot tops, cilantro, garlic, lemon zest, and salt.

5. To assemble: Spread the labaneh over the bottom of a shallow bowl and lay the warm carrots on top. Drizzle with the reserved honey harissa, dollop with the gremolata, sprinkle with some flaky salt, and finish with a drizzle of olive oil and a scattering of cilantro.

hot new side piece

CHAPTER 6

boss
veg

I think one thing that holds people back from cooking more vegetarian meals is the idea that they won't be filling or satisfying—or that they just straight up won't be as good as the usual meaty go-tos. Well, this chapter is about to prove that wrong about fourteen different ways. By celebrating veg and their natural features; throwing caution to the wind when it comes to piling on the flavors and **saucy**, **crispy**, **gooey**, **creamy**, **crunchy** textures; and leaning way, way into condiments, you can absolutely end up with a dish that holds its own on the table. And not just that—no one will leave feeling like they missed the meat.

caramelized shallot and hawaij maqloubeh

Serves 4

FOR THE RICE

⅓ cup extra-virgin olive oil

1 (15-ounce) can chickpeas, drained, rinsed, and dried well

2 teaspoons Savory Hawaij (page 24) or curry powder

2½ teaspoons kosher salt

Freshly ground black pepper to taste

1 medium yellow onion, chopped

2 medium garlic cloves, finely chopped

1½ cups basmati rice, rinsed until the water runs clear

2 cups vegetable stock or water

½ cup golden raisins

FOR THE CARAMELIZED SHALLOTS

¼ cup extra-virgin olive oil

4 tablespoons (½ stick) unsalted butter

8 medium shallots, peeled and halved

Kosher salt and freshly ground black pepper to taste

1 teaspoon sugar

Juice of 1 lemon

FOR SERVING

Full-fat Greek yogurt

Maqloubeh, or Palestinian "upside-down" rice, is a classic preparation in which meat, vegetables, and rice are simmered in a spiced broth. The best part is when you turn it all out onto a platter for an impressive presentation that looks like the world's most stunning savory upside-down cake. This is my (loose) vegetarian interpretation, which has the same rich, stew-y flavor from caramelized shallots plus a cameo from Yemeni hawaij.

1. Make the rice: Heat the olive oil in a medium pot over medium-high heat. When the oil shimmers, add the chickpeas and fry until almost crisp, about 4 minutes. Season with the hawaij, salt, and a couple cracks of pepper and continue frying until crispy, about 2 more minutes.

2. Add the onion and garlic and fry until softened and lightly golden, stirring occasionally, about 5 minutes. Stir in the rice and stock and allow the pot to come to a boil. Cover and reduce the heat to medium. After 5 minutes, turn off the heat and add the raisins. Fluff the rice with a fork and set aside until ready to assemble.

3. Make the shallots: Heat the olive oil and butter in a medium nonstick pan with a fitted lid over medium heat. (I like a deep 8-inch skillet for this.) When the butter melts and begins to foam, add the shallots and season well with salt and pepper. Arrange the shallots cut side down and cook until golden, about 8 minutes. Use a metal spatula to carefully flip the shallots so they stay together, season again, and brown on the second side, about 5 minutes.

4. Add ⅓ cup of water to the pan and cover. Reduce the heat to low and cook until the shallots are tender and deeply golden, 20 to 25 minutes.

recipe continues

Sprinkle the shallots with the sugar and carefully flip them again so they're cut side down.

5. Spread the partially cooked rice over the shallots and pour 1 cup of water over the top. Cover and cook over medium-low heat until the rice has fluffed, 20 to 25 minutes.

6. Squeeze the lemon over the rice before placing a large serving plate over the top and inverting the whole thing. Let the pan sit for a minute to allow everything to release onto the plate. (And if it doesn't, no worries; just stick the shallots back on top.) Serve hot with yogurt.

summertime (or anytime) stewed veggie couscous

Serves 4 to 6

¼ cup extra-virgin olive oil

2 large yellow onions, finely diced

2 tablespoons Fast 'n' Fresh Harissa (page 33; see Notes, page 176)

1 teaspoon ground turmeric

1 teaspoon ground cumin

1 teaspoon ground coriander

Kosher salt and freshly ground black pepper to taste

6 medium garlic cloves, finely chopped

3 large carrots, peeled and sliced into ¾-inch chunks

2 Russet potatoes (or Yukon Gold or sweet potatoes or anything you have on hand), peeled and chopped into 1-inch pieces

1 celeriac root, peeled and chopped into ¾-inch pieces (optional, see Notes, page 176)

3 celery ribs, chopped into large chunks

⅓ cup tomato paste or 1 (15-ounce) can tomato sauce

8 cups vegetable stock or water

2 medium zucchini, sliced into ¾-inch-thick rounds

1 (15-ounce) can chickpeas, drained and rinsed

One bite of this classic dish and I'm right back on the beach in Herzliya, Israel. After hanging out in the water all day, we'd stay for dinner at a local restaurant where the tables were right on the beach. My sisters and I would play in the sand between bites of fresh, fluffy, veggie-studded couscous, our fingers still salty from the sea. It somehow managed to be the ultimate comfort food and yet light enough for dinner when your skin is still warm from the afternoon sun. Now I frequently make this at home, and the leftovers are a welcome sight in my fridge all week because the flavors continue to deepen as it sits.

1. Heat the olive oil in a large pot over medium heat. When the oil shimmers, add the onions and sauté, stirring occasionally, until translucent, 3 to 5 minutes. Stir in the harissa, turmeric, cumin, and coriander and season with a healthy pinch of salt and a few cracks of pepper. Add the garlic and cook until the spices have released their fragrance, about 1 minute.

2. Add the carrots, potatoes, celeriac (if using), and celery and stir in the tomato paste to coat the vegetables. Cook, stirring occasionally, until the tomato paste darkens in color (or about 2 minutes, if using tomato sauce). Pour in the stock and season again (well!) with salt and pepper.

3. Increase the heat to medium-high and bring the pot to a boil. Reduce the heat to medium and allow it to simmer for 30 minutes. Taste and add more salt and pepper, if needed, then add the zucchini and chickpeas. Simmer for another 30 minutes, until the vegetables are tender and the flavors have melded.

recipe and ingredients continue

My Lazy (and Awesomely Delicious and Versatile) Couscous (recipe follows) or 4 cups cooked instant couscous (see Notes), for serving

Fresh soft herbs for garnish, such as parsley, cilantro, or dill (optional)

Notes: If you're not into heat, either reduce the amount of harissa here or leave it out altogether.

Feel free to sub in your favorite veggies or whatever you have lying around in the veg drawer. Just remember to toss in denser vegetables first and save the more tender veg for later (the same way I add the carrots and potatoes earlier, then the zucchini toward the end).

I love serving this over my "lazy couscous," which is like one effort notch above instant, but if instant is all that's in the cards for you, be sure to add a good knob of butter in there too.

4. Check for seasoning once more, then pour the vegetables and sauce over couscous. Finish with herbs, if desired.

my lazy (and awesomely delicious and versatile) couscous

This is the perfect base to play with all kinds of mix-ins like chopped dates or raisins; a pinch of ground turmeric, saffron, or other spices; and fresh herbs—let your couscous freak flag fly.

MAKES ABOUT 4 CUPS

8 tablespoons (1 stick) unsalted butter

Pinch of ground cinnamon

2½ cups vegetable stock or water

2 cups instant couscous

Kosher salt to taste

1. In a small pot over medium heat, combine the butter and cinnamon. This is when you'd add any other spices you wanted to experiment with. Stir to combine and let the butter melt. Add the stock and bring to a boil. Turn off the heat, add the couscous, and mix well.

2. Cover the pot and let the couscous steam for 5 minutes. Fluff with a fork and season with salt before serving. (Or add any other mix-ins.)

3. To store the couscous in the fridge for future meals, let it cool completely before transferring it to an airtight container for up to 5 days.

eggplant schnitzel with spiced harissa tomato sauce and garlicky tahini

Serves 4 to 6

2 medium eggplants, ends trimmed, cut lengthwise into ¼-inch-thick slices

Kosher salt to taste

½ cup all-purpose flour

½ cup cornstarch

Freshly ground black pepper to taste

3 large eggs

1½ cups panko bread crumbs

1 cup refined avocado or grapeseed oil

Spiced Harissa Tomato Sauce (page 270), for serving

Garlicky Tahini (page 59), for serving

Fresh basil leaves, for serving

This preparation felt almost too obvious because the Italians kind of got there first (hey, eggplant Parm), but the idea of schnitzel-fying soft, sweet eggplant was just too good to pass up. So I gave it a Middle Eastern glow-up with harissa-spiced tomato sauce and way too much (yet never enough) garlicky tahini. It brings it, and it brings it so good.

1. Arrange the eggplant slices in a single layer on a paper towel–lined cutting board or baking sheet and sprinkle with salt. Let the eggplant sit for 20 minutes, then pat dry with a clean towel.

2. Meanwhile, in a medium shallow bowl, stir together the flour and cornstarch and season well with salt and pepper. In another medium bowl, beat the eggs and season with salt and pepper. And on a large plate, add the panko and season well with salt and pepper.

3. Dredge the dried eggplant slices through the flour mixture and tap off any excess. Coat the eggplant in the egg, letting any excess drip off. Finish with a coating of panko, making sure to really press it into the eggplant.

4. Line a large plate with paper towels.

5. Heat the oil in a large skillet over medium-high heat. When the oil shimmers, add enough eggplant slices to fit comfortably in a single layer without crowding the pan. Fry until the first side is golden brown, 3 to 4 minutes. Flip and repeat on the second side, 2 to 3 minutes. Transfer the eggplant to the prepared plate and immediately sprinkle with salt. Repeat with the remaining eggplant slices.

6. Serve the eggplant with the tomato sauce, tahini, and basil.

ultimate shroom shawarma

Serves 4 to 6

6 tablespoons extra-virgin olive oil

Juice of 1 lemon

3 medium garlic cloves, grated

1 tablespoon shawarma spice
or curry powder (see Note)

1 teaspoon Fast 'n' Fresh Harissa
(page 33; optional)

1 teaspoon ground cumin

1 teaspoon ground coriander

1 teaspoon paprika

1 teaspoon kosher salt, plus more
to taste

½ teaspoon ground turmeric

Freshly ground black pepper
to taste

2 pounds mixed mushrooms (I like
oyster, cremini, king, and shiitake)

2 small yellow onions, finely sliced

FOR SERVING (ALL OPTIONAL)

Laffa (page 236), pita, or rice

Garlicky Tahini (page 59)

Chopped Salad (page 53)

Celery Zhoug (page 30)

Golden Amba Pepper Sauce
(page 34)

Preserved Lemon Toum (page 41)

Rinsed and chopped rind of
Preserved Lemon (page 67)

Israeli Pickles (page 37)

Fresh parsley, for garnish

If I had to pick THE dish I run to when I land in Israel, it would be shawarma—or juicy spiced meat piled on a fluffy pita cloud, topped with chopped salad, and doused with *alllll* the condiments. I had to include a version in this book, namely because it felt like the ultimate challenge to re-create that deep, savory, meaty satisfaction with veg. The obvious choice was mushrooms, which come in a wide variety of tastes and textures and take on flavor really well, especially when they're tossed with thinly sliced onion, coated in spices, and caramelized until they're melt-in-your-mouth tender. You could really use this recipe anywhere meat is called for.

1. In a large bowl, stir together 2 tablespoons of the olive oil plus the lemon juice, garlic, shawarma spice, harissa (if using), cumin, coriander, paprika, salt, turmeric, and a few cracks of pepper.

2. Make sure all the mushrooms are about the same size, tearing any larger mushrooms into slightly smaller pieces, if necessary. Add them to the bowl and use your hands to really slather them in the seasoning mixture. Set aside.

3. Heat 2 more tablespoons of the olive oil in a large skillet over medium-high heat. When the oil shimmers, add the onions and season well with salt and pepper. Sauté until lightly golden, about 5 minutes. Transfer the onions to a medium bowl and set aside.

4. To the same pan over medium-high heat, add half of the mushroom mixture, drizzle with another 1 tablespoon of the olive oil, and season with salt and pepper. Sear, not touching the mushrooms, until they have a deep golden crust, about 2 minutes. Flip the mushrooms and repeat on the other side, another 2 minutes. Transfer the mushrooms to

the bowl with the onions and repeat with the remaining mushrooms, adding the remaining 1 tablespoon olive oil.

5. Serve bundled up in laffa or pita or heaped over rice topped with chopped salad and any/all of the condiments.

Note: If you happen to have a shawarma spice blend in your pantry (like mine from *Eating Out Loud*), use that, but if you can't find it, curry powder is a great substitution.

charred beets with honey caraway lentils and tzatziki

Serves 4 to 6

FOR THE BEETS

6 medium red and yellow beets, scrubbed

2 tablespoons extra-virgin olive oil

1 teaspoon kosher salt

FOR THE HONEY CARAWAY LENTILS

3 tablespoons extra-virgin olive oil, plus more for serving

Juice of ½ lemon

1 tablespoon honey

2 teaspoons champagne vinegar

1 teaspoon caraway or cumin seeds, toasted in a dry pan until fragrant

1 teaspoon kosher salt, plus more to taste

Freshly ground black pepper to taste

¾ cup cooked French lentils

FOR SERVING

1½ cups Tzatziki (page 73)

Flaky sea salt

⅓ cup slivered almonds, toasted in a dry pan until fragrant

4 Medjool dates, pitted and finely chopped

Fresh dill

Hot take, but beets are one of my favorite vegetables. To the point where, yes, a similar version of this recipe was included in my last book, but honestly, some ingredients just belong together. Also I pride myself on finding ways for people to love them as much as I do, and this is what's going to get you there. This dish is all about how succulent and meat-like they get when roasted until tender and charred. You could just serve them on a bed of homemade garlicky tzatziki and be very satisfied, but if you also balance the beets' natural earthiness with lentils that have been brought to life with caraway, vinegar, dates, and almonds, you'll be a convert for life. It's messy and dribbly and yet perfectly elegant—my kind of dish.

1. Preheat the oven to 400°F.

2. Make the beets: Arrange the beets on a baking sheet and toss with the olive oil, salt, and 2 tablespoons of water. Cover with foil and roast for about 30 minutes, until a knife easily slides into the beets. Remove the foil and continue roasting until the beets caramelize and char a bit, about 10 more minutes. Set aside to cool.

3. While the beets cool, make the lentils: In a medium bowl, stir together the olive oil, lemon juice, honey, vinegar, caraway, and salt, plus a couple cracks of black pepper. Add the lentils and mix to combine, seasoning with more salt and/or pepper, if needed.

4. When the beets are cool enough to handle, slice them into ½-inch-thick slices.

5. To serve: Spread the tzatziki over a serving plate, lay the sliced beets on top, pour on the lentils, and season with a sprinkle of flaky salt.

6. Finish with a scattering of the almonds and dates, a drizzle of olive oil, and the dill.

root steaks with chilichurri

FOR THE STEAKS

3 celeriac roots, peeled

2 large watermelon radishes, peeled (see Note)

3 tablespoons extra-virgin olive oil

1 teaspoon kosher salt, plus more as needed

Freshly ground black pepper to taste

2 tablespoons unsalted butter

FOR THE CHILICHURRI

1 cup chopped fresh cilantro leaves

½ cup extra-virgin olive oil

1 tablespoon red wine vinegar

1 fresh cayenne chile or your favorite hot pepper (adjusting size based on its heat and removing the seeds if less heat is desired), finely sliced (optional)

Kosher salt and freshly ground black pepper to taste

FOR SERVING

1 cup Garlicky Tahini (page 59)

Roasting low and slow isn't just for large cuts of meat. When you give root vegetables like celeriac or whole watermelon radishes what I like to think of as the brisket treatment, you end up with a veg transformed. They're tender yet meaty with real body, almost like you're cutting into a steak. So I figured why not really go there by drizzling over a "chilichurri," which is basically chimichurri, an herby, oily, vinegar-spiked condiment that I've loaded up with fresh chiles. (You could technically omit them if you're not into the heat, but I personally am here for the spice.) Give the whole thing a schmear of garlicky tahini and devour.

1. Preheat the oven to 300°F.

2. Make the steaks: Place the whole celeriac and radishes in the bottom of a large Dutch oven. Drizzle with 2 tablespoons of the olive oil and season with the salt. Cover and roast for 2 hours, until you can easily slide a knife through. Set aside to cool slightly.

3. While the vegetables roast, make the chilichurri: In a medium bowl, whisk together the cilantro, olive oil, vinegar, and chile (if using). Season with salt and pepper and set aside.

4. Cut the celeriac and radishes into ½-inch-thick slices. Season on both sides with salt and pepper.

5. Heat the remaining 1 tablespoon olive oil and the butter in a large skillet over medium-high heat. When the butter has melted and is starting to foam, add enough vegetable slices to fit comfortably in one layer without crowding the pan. Sear until golden, about 3 minutes. Flip and sear the second side until golden, about another 3 minutes. Transfer the steaks to a plate and repeat with the remaining vegetable slices.

6. **To serve:** Spread the tahini over a serving plate, layer the steaks on top, and drizzle with the chilichurri.

Note: If you can't find watermelon radishes, you could sub in rutabaga, turnips, or kohlrabi.

eggplant with sumac and labaneh

⅓ cup plus ¼ cup extra-virgin olive oil

3 medium garlic cloves, finely grated

1 tablespoon rinsed and finely chopped rind of Preserved Lemons (page 67)

1 tablespoon honey

1 tablespoon ground sumac, plus more for serving

1 tablespoon Aleppo pepper or red chile flakes

½ teaspoon kosher salt, plus more to taste

3 medium eggplants

1 cup Labaneh (page 42)

Flaky sea salt, for serving

Fresh flat-leaf parsley leaves, for serving

Fresh cilantro leaves, for serving

½ lime

Laffa (page 236), for serving

At the end of the day, roasted eggplant is a superior vegetable experience; it's savory and smoky and indulgently steak-y. Imagine how magical things get when you infuse it with some chile and garlic heat, citrusy sumac, and sunbeams of preserved lemon plus a schmear of tangy labaneh. It's light and luscious bliss worthy of a special-meal moment. Trust.

1. Preheat the oven to 450°F. Line a baking sheet with parchment paper.

2. In a medium bowl, stir together ⅓ cup of the olive oil with the garlic, preserved lemon, honey, sumac, Aleppo, and salt. Set aside.

3. Trim both ends of each eggplant and slice in half lengthwise. Use the tip of your knife to slice diagonal lines into the flesh of the eggplant about 1 inch apart, taking care to not cut all the way through (but don't freak out if you do). Now make diagonal lines going the opposite way to make a crosshatch pattern.

4. Arrange the eggplant halves on the prepared baking sheet cut side up. Drizzle the remaining ¼ cup olive oil over the eggplant and season with a generous pinch of salt.

5. Roast for 30 minutes, then flip the eggplant and cook until completely tender and golden, 15 to 20 more minutes.

6. Remove the eggplant from the oven and flip once more so the halves are again cut side up. Spoon the sumac mixture over the eggplant and return it to the oven for another 10 minutes, until nicely golden.

7. Spread the labaneh on a serving plate and lay the eggplant on top. Finish with another pinch of sumac and flaky salt plus parsley and cilantro. Squeeze the lime over the top and eat warm with laffa.

hawaij sweet potatoes with roasted lemon relish and yogurt

FOR THE HAWAIJ SWEET POTATOES

1 lemon, scrubbed and halved

6 medium sweet potatoes, scrubbed and halved lengthwise

¼ cup extra-virgin olive oil

1 teaspoon Savory Hawaij (page 24) or curry powder

½ teaspoon ground cumin

1 teaspoon kosher salt

Freshly ground black pepper to taste

FOR THE ROASTED LEMON RELISH

½ cup extra-virgin olive oil

¼ cup fresh mint leaves, finely chopped

¼ cup fresh flat-leaf parsley leaves, finely chopped

1 jalapeño, seeded and minced (optional)

1 small shallot, minced

1 small garlic clove, finely chopped

¾ teaspoon kosher salt

Freshly ground black pepper to taste

FOR THE YOGURT

1½ cups full-fat Greek yogurt

2 tablespoons fresh lemon juice (about ½ lemon)

Flaky sea salt to taste

As we talked about in chapter 1, hawaij is a Yemeni ground spice mixture that transforms everything it touches into golden savory exquisiteness. I wondered what would happen if I gave sweet potatoes a hawaij body scrub before roasting them, and sure enough, the result was just as rich, creamy, sweet, and savory as I'd hoped it would be.

1. Preheat the oven to 425°F. Line a baking sheet with parchment paper.

2. Make the sweet potatoes: Slice one of the lemon halves into ¼-inch-thick rings. Set aside.

3. In a small bowl, stir together the olive oil, hawaij, and ground cumin. Place the sweet potatoes, lemon rings, and half lemon on the prepared baking sheet and coat with the hawaij oil. Season with the salt and a few cracks of pepper and place everything cut side down. Roast for 20 minutes, until the lemons are golden, then remove the lemons and continue roasting the sweet potatoes for another 15 to 20 minutes, until they are tender, browned, and charred in spots. Allow everything to cool slightly.

4. Make the relish: Finely chop the roasted lemon rings. In a medium bowl, combine the chopped lemon with the olive oil, mint, parsley, jalapeño (if using), shallot, garlic, salt, and a few cracks of pepper. Toss to combine and set aside.

5. Make the yogurt: In a medium bowl, stir together the yogurt and lemon juice. Season with a good pinch of flaky salt.

6. To serve: Dollop the yogurt onto a platter. Place the roasted sweet potatoes on top and finish with the relish, cumin seeds, and herbs. Serve with the remaining roasted lemon half for squeezing over everything.

FOR SERVING

1 teaspoon cumin seeds, toasted
in a dry pan until fragrant

Fresh mint and/or parsley leaves

squash and walnut kibbeh with tahini, sumac, and lemon

Makes 12 kibbeh (serves 4)

1 medium butternut squash, peeled and chopped (see Note, page 192)

6 cups plus 1 tablespoon refined avocado or grapeseed oil

2 teaspoons kosher salt, plus more to taste

Freshly ground black pepper to taste

1 cup fine bulgur

2 tablespoons extra-virgin olive oil

1 large yellow onion, finely chopped

3 medium garlic cloves, finely grated

1 tablespoon Baharat (page 20)

1 large egg

¼ cup all-purpose flour

½ cup raw walnuts, toasted in a dry pan until fragrant and roughly chopped

Sumac, for serving

1 lemon, quartered

Garlicky Tahini (page 59), for serving

Preserved Lemon Toum (page 41), for serving

A couple years ago, I went on a food crawl through Israel with one of my best friends, Tali. The real stand-out moment was when we went to the restaurant Haj Kahil in Jaffa, and they brought out a piping-hot batch of kibbeh (also called kubbeh in Israel), torpedo-shaped parcels of meat and nuts encased in a crispy bulgur shell that are considered to be the national dish of Lebanon and Syria. But if you swap the meat for rich butternut squash and add baharat-spiced onions, you get a veg version that can go toe to toe with the original any day. No need to involve any silverware here—just pick these up with your hands, dip in your sauces, and shove in your mouth.

1. Preheat the oven to 425°F.

2. Spread the butternut squash over a baking sheet. Drizzle with 1 tablespoon of the avocado oil, season with a good pinch of salt and a couple cracks of pepper, and use your hands to coat the squash well. Roast for 40 to 45 minutes, until lightly golden and easily pierced with a knife.

3. While the squash is baking, bundle the bulgur in a piece of cheesecloth and submerge it in a bowl of water for 15 minutes, until it has plumped up. Lift the bundle from the bowl and squeeze out as much liquid as possible. (Alternatively, you could put the bulgur in a fine-mesh strainer and submerge it, then use a spatula to press out the water.) Set aside.

4. Heat the olive oil in a large skillet over medium-high heat. When the oil shimmers, add the onion, season with 1 teaspoon of the salt and a couple cracks of pepper, and sauté, stirring occasionally, until just softened, about 2 minutes. Stir in the garlic and baharat and reduce the heat to medium-low. Cook,

recipe continues

Note: You can substitute 2 medium sweet potatoes for the butternut squash.

stirring occasionally, until the onions are lightly golden, 10 to 15 minutes. Remove the pan from the heat and set aside.

5. Add the squash to a food processor and pulse until it is broken down but not completely creamy. Measure out 1 cup of the puree and add it to a large bowl. Measure out ½ cup of the puree and add it to a medium bowl. (That should be just about how much puree you have.)

6. To the large bowl of squash, add the bulgur, half of the onion mixture, the egg, flour, ½ teaspoon of the salt, and a couple cracks of pepper. Stir to combine and set aside.

7. To the medium bowl, add the remaining onion mixture, the walnuts, the remaining ½ teaspoon salt, and a couple cracks of pepper. Stir to combine and season with more salt, if needed.

8. Use a ¼-cup measuring cup to make 12 portions of the bulgur mixture. Using damp hands, take each ball and gently press to flatten it in your palm. Fill the flattened ball with 1 tablespoon of the walnut mixture, then pinch the edges of the bulgur mixture over the

filling and mold it into an oval shape with points on the ends as you gently tighten the casing around the filling.

9. Place the finished kibbeh on a plate and refrigerate them for at least 2 hours or up to 2 days.

10. When ready to cook, heat the remaining 6 cups avocado oil in a medium pot over medium-high heat. You want the oil to reach at least halfway up the pan. Line a large plate with paper towels.

11. When the oil reaches 375°F on a candy thermometer, or a small bit of the kibbeh mixture immediately bubbles when it hits the oil, carefully add four or five kibbeh to the pot.

12. Use a kitchen spider or slotted spoon to continuously turn each kibbeh so it fries evenly until it has a beautiful dark crust on all sides, 3 to 5 minutes total. Transfer the finished kibbeh to the lined plate and immediately sprinkle with salt. Continue with the remaining kibbeh.

13. Serve hot sprinkled with sumac alongside lemon wedges, garlicky tahini, and preserved lemon toum.

arayes

lebanese stuffed pitas with cauliflower, mushrooms, and walnuts

Makes 6 pitas (serves 6 to 12)

½ cup extra-virgin olive oil, plus more for brushing

2 teaspoons ground cumin

1 teaspoon smoked paprika

½ teaspoon cayenne pepper

3 teaspoons kosher salt

½ teaspoon freshly ground black pepper

1 small head cauliflower, stem trimmed, cut into bite-size pieces

1 pound mixed mushrooms (I like oyster and shiitake), torn in half

1 medium yellow onion, minced

½ cup raw walnut halves, roughly chopped

½ cup fresh flat-leaf parsley, finely chopped

4 medium garlic cloves, minced

6 pitas, halved

Fresh herbs such as parsley or cilantro, for serving

Celery Zhoug (page 30), for serving

Garlicky Tahini (page 59), for serving

I first had the "original" version of this traditional Middle Eastern street food dish at a restaurant called M25 in Tel Aviv. They'd stuffed a fluffy pita with ground seasoned lamb, then seared the whole thing on a charcoal grill so the bread soaked up all the juices and every bite had big smoky flavor. Then you'd go to town with your favorite condiments. There was no way this book wasn't going to include a veg'd-out version, so to do it real justice, I had to call in the big guns: mushrooms, cauliflower, walnuts, and spices like cumin, cayenne, and smoked paprika. The craveability factor remains exactly the same and so does the objective: stuff, sauce, inhale.

1. Preheat a grill pan or cast-iron skillet over medium-high heat (see Note, page 194).

2. In a small bowl, stir together the olive oil, cumin, paprika, cayenne, 2 teaspoons of the salt, and the black pepper.

3. Arrange the cauliflower and mushroom pieces on a baking sheet, drizzle with the spiced oil, and use your hands to coat the vegetables well and really get into the crannies.

4. Sear the vegetables in the pan, working in batches if necessary, until they're tender and charred in spots and release easily from the pan, 4 to 5 minutes. Use tongs to rotate them so they cook evenly. Return the finished vegetables to the baking sheet and reserve the pan for cooking the pitas.

5. Reserve 2 cups of the grilled mushrooms in a large bowl and set aside. Give the remaining

recipe continues

Note: You could also make this on a grill at the same temperatures as written. It'll be delicious and smoky, but you'll have to be gentle and take care not to let the arayes fall apart on you.

mushrooms a rough chop. Add the chopped mushrooms and all the cauliflower to a large bowl with the onion, walnuts, parsley, garlic, and the remaining 1 teaspoon salt. Toss to combine.

6. Working in two to three batches, transfer the mixture to a food processor and pulse until the mixture just holds together but still has texture. Add the filling to the bowl with the reserved mushrooms and fold to combine.

7. Divide the filling among the pita pockets, filling each to the top and using your fingers to really press the filling into the edges. Brush the outside of the pita and top of the filling with olive oil.

8. Heat the reserved pan over high heat and add two pitas at a time, placing the side with the exposed filling down. Cook until nicely charred, 2 to 3 minutes, then flip to char the two sides, 2 to 3 minutes per side. Repeat with the remaining pitas.

9. Serve hot scattered with fresh herbs and with zhoug and tahini for dipping.

harissa-roasted cauliflower and broccoli with golden raisin gremolata and toum

FOR THE ROASTED CAULIFLOWER AND BROCCOLI

¼ cup extra-virgin olive oil

¼ cup Fast 'n' Fresh Harissa (page 33)

1 medium head cauliflower, stem trimmed to 3 inches, cut into 6 pieces

1 medium head broccoli, stem trimmed to 3 inches, cut into 6 pieces

1 teaspoon kosher salt

FOR THE GOLDEN RAISIN GREMOLATA

1 cup chopped fresh flat-leaf parsley

½ cup plus 2 tablespoons extra-virgin olive oil

½ cup roasted hazelnuts, chopped

½ cup golden raisins, soaked in water for 10 minutes, drained, and chopped

¼ cup brined capers, drained

2 teaspoons grated lemon zest

Kosher salt to taste

FOR SERVING

Preserved Lemon Toum (page 41)

I don't think you can ever go wrong with roasted cauliflower, but I think I speak for all of us when I say that sometimes she deserves a little dressing up. To transform this veg staple into a main dish worthy of the spotlight, I pulled out all the stops: it gets rubbed down with harissa before roasting to peak caramelization; heaped with fresh herbs, capers, and raisins; and served with plenty of garlicky, lemony toum for mopping up. And to bring a little more texture and color to the mix, I threw in broccoli too. But you could use all of one or the other, if you'd prefer.

1. Preheat the oven to 500°F.

2. Make the cauliflower and broccoli: In a small bowl, stir together the olive oil and harissa.

3. Arrange the cauliflower and broccoli on a baking sheet and drizzle with the harissa oil. Use your hands to rub it into the vegetables, making sure to get into all the crannies. Season all over with the salt.

4. Roast for about 30 minutes, until the vegetables are golden and charred in spots.

5. While the cauliflower and broccoli roast, make the gremolata: In a medium bowl, stir together the parsley, olive oil, hazelnuts, raisins, capers, lemon zest, and a pinch of salt.

6. Arrange the roasted veg on a platter and drizzle with the gremolata. Serve with a bowl of toum for dipping.

fennel tagine with olives and preserved lemons

Serves 4 to 6

½ cup extra-virgin olive oil, plus more as needed

2 large yellow onions, finely chopped

1 teaspoon kosher salt, plus more to taste

4 medium garlic cloves, finely chopped

1 tablespoon grated fresh ginger

1 teaspoon coriander seeds, toasted in a dry pan until fragrant

1 teaspoon fennel seeds, toasted in a dry pan until fragrant

1 teaspoon Aleppo pepper or red chile flakes

6 medium fennel bulbs, trimmed and halved (reserve any fronds for garnish)

Freshly ground black pepper to taste

2 large Yukon Gold potatoes, peeled and cut into 1-inch chunks (see Note)

4 cups vegetable stock or water

1 cup pitted Castelvetrano olives

⅓ cup black raisins or currants

2 tablespoons rinsed and chopped rind of Preserved Lemons (page 67)

⅓ cup chopped fresh cilantro leaves, plus more for garnish

4 cups cooked instant couscous or basmati rice, for serving

Moroccan tagine is something I come back to over and over again in my cooking. There's something so cozy and comforting about a simple braise with garlic and spices, and all that rich succulence punctuated with bright bursts of olives and preserved lemons. This all-veg version has fennel as the main attraction, and let me tell you, when it cooks down into the sweetest, most tender version of itself and soaks up all that flavor, it becomes much more special than something you just threw in a pan. Spooned over couscous or rice, this could be dressed up for company, or you could take down a bowl or two while curled up on the couch.

1. Heat ¼ cup of the olive oil in a large Dutch oven over medium heat. Add the onions and salt and sauté, stirring occasionally, until translucent and golden in places, 10 to 12 minutes.

2. Stir in the garlic, ginger, coriander, fennel seeds, and Aleppo and sauté just long enough for everything to become fragrant, 1 to 2 minutes. Transfer the onion mixture to a bowl and set aside.

3. In the same pot over medium-high heat, heat the remaining ¼ cup olive oil. Add the fennel bulbs, season with salt and black pepper, and sear, flipping occasionally, until golden on all sides, about 5 minutes per side. Add more oil to the pan if needed.

4. Return the onion mixture to the pot, then add the potatoes and season with salt. Pour in the stock and allow the pot to come to a boil, using a wooden spoon to scrape up all the browned bits from the bottom of the pot. Cover, reduce the heat to medium-low, and simmer for 20 minutes. Stir in the olives, raisins, and preserved lemon and simmer uncovered for 15 more minutes, until the potatoes are

Note: To make this dish even heartier and add more protein, you can add one 15-ounce can drained and rinsed chickpeas to the dish when you add the potatoes.

tender and the flavors have melded.

5. Stir in the cilantro, season with more salt if needed, and serve over hot couscous or rice. Finish with more cilantro and fennel fronds (if you have them).

herb-stuffed peppers in black lime sauce

Serves 8

FOR THE FILLING AND PEPPERS

2 tablespoons plus
2½ teaspoons kosher salt,
plus more to taste

1½ cups basmati rice, rinsed until
the water runs clear

3 tablespoons extra-virgin
olive oil

2 large yellow onions, finely
diced

3 medium garlic cloves, finely
diced

2 teaspoons ground turmeric

Large pinch of saffron threads

Freshly ground black pepper
to taste

1 (15-ounce) can kidney beans,
drained and rinsed

1 (15-ounce) can chickpeas,
drained and rinsed

½ cup chopped fresh cilantro

½ cup chopped fresh flat-leaf
parsley leaves

½ cup chopped fresh dill

8 medium bell peppers
(red, yellow, and orange)

When I was growing up, stuffed peppers were a staple in our home. I have a vivid memory—and a home video to prove it—of my first cousin Chen and me playing at our summer cottage when we were about seven years old, begging our moms for stuffed peppers for dinner. This Ashkenazi Jewish comfort food classic isn't much more than bell peppers stuffed with rice and ground beef with a beautiful tomato sauce, but the overall effect of these elements simmered together is transformative (in taste and in spirit). And to be perfectly honest, the meat is beside the point. Instead, I've subbed in beans—the easiest, least expensive, most flavor-absorbing hack there is—and given the whole thing a Persian-inspired twist. Saffron, garlic, and fresh herbs perfume the filling, while dried lime lifts and brightens the sauce. It's just as hearty and homey as the original, but with a little extra something special.

1. Make the filling and peppers: Bring a large pot of water to a boil over medium-high heat and season with 2 tablespoons of the salt. Add the rice and boil until the rice is al dente, 3 to 5 minutes. Drain, add to a large bowl, and set aside.

2. Heat the olive oil in a large skillet over medium-high heat. Add the onions and the remaining 2½ teaspoons salt, the garlic, turmeric, saffron, and a couple cracks of black pepper. Sauté, stirring occasionally, until the onions have softened, about 2 minutes. Transfer the mixture to the bowl with the rice and mix well. Add the kidney beans, chickpeas, cilantro, parsley, and dill, stir to combine, and season with more salt, if needed. You really want that flavor to pop.

recipe and ingredients continue

boss veg

201

FOR THE SAUCE

2 tablespoons extra-virgin olive oil

1 large yellow onion, finely diced

2 medium garlic cloves, finely diced

2 teaspoons kosher salt

1 teaspoon ground turmeric

¼ teaspoon ground cinnamon

Pinch of saffron threads

Freshly ground black pepper to taste

½ cup tomato paste

1 (28-ounce) can crushed tomatoes (I like San Marzano)

3 dried black limes, pierced a few times with a fork or knife (see Note, page 147)

3. Slice off the top of each bell pepper and pull out the ribs and seeds. Divide the rice mixture among the peppers, really filling them to the top. Set aside while you make the sauce or store in a sealed container in the fridge for up to 2 days.

4. Make the sauce: Heat the olive oil in a large Dutch oven over medium-high heat. Add the onion, garlic, salt, turmeric, cinnamon, saffron, and a couple cracks of black pepper. Sauté, stirring occasionally, until the onions have softened, about 2 minutes. Add the tomato paste and cook, stirring, until it darkens in color, about 2 minutes. Pour in the crushed tomatoes, fill the can to the top with water, and pour that in as well. Add the dried limes and let the pot come to a boil. Turn off the heat.

5. Add half of the sauce to a second large pot, then nestle the peppers in the bottom of both the Dutch oven and the second pot. Spoon the sauce over the tops of the peppers in both pots. Bring the sauce to a boil in both pots over medium-high heat, cover, and reduce the heat to medium-low. Let things simmer until the peppers are completely soft and the flavors have melded, 45 minutes to 1 hour. Serve hot and sauced.

saucy "meatballs"

Makes about 16 "meatballs" (serves 4)

FOR THE BALLS

½ medium yellow onion, roughly chopped

¼ cup chopped fresh cilantro leaves, plus more for serving

¼ cup chopped fresh flat-leaf parsley leaves

3 medium garlic cloves

1 cup canned chickpeas, drained, rinsed, and dried

¾ cup cooked quinoa or cracked bulgur

½ cup panko bread crumbs

2 large eggs

1½ teaspoons kosher salt

1 teaspoon paprika

½ teaspoon ground cumin

½ teaspoon ground coriander

½ teaspoon ground turmeric

⅓ cup extra-virgin olive oil

FOR THE SAUCE

3 tablespoons extra-virgin olive oil

1 medium yellow onion, finely chopped

1½ teaspoons kosher salt

¼ teaspoon freshly ground black pepper

2 medium garlic cloves, grated

1 teaspoon ground turmeric

I knew I needed to include a meatball in this book because everywhere you go in Israel you see ktzitzot, which are pretty much your run-of-the-mill (but intensely tasty) chicken, lamb, fish, or beef meatballs. So, my first order of business was coming up with the ultimate vegetarian ball that's equally delicious and doesn't fall apart on you: check and check. And while you can enjoy ktzitzot on rice or tucked into a pita, my favorite way to have them is simmered in a spiced tomatoey sauce, which is why I've given you that option. But these would be the perfect centerpiece for any spread, whether you're eating them with laffa or basmati rice, over polenta, or out of a bowl. They're just a fantastic, versatile "meat" ball.

1. Make the balls: In a food processor, combine the onion, cilantro, parsley, and garlic. Pulse until finely chopped but not mushy. Transfer the mixture to a fine-mesh sieve and press out as much liquid as possible. Transfer the mixture to a large bowl and set aside.

2. Add the chickpeas to the food processor (no need to wipe it out first) and pulse a few times until finely chopped, but again, not mushy. Transfer the chopped chickpeas to the fine-mesh sieve and press out any liquid, then add the chickpeas

to the bowl with the onion mixture.

3. Stir in the quinoa, panko, eggs, salt, paprika, cumin, coriander, and turmeric until well incorporated.

4. Line a baking sheet with parchment paper.

5. Form the mixture into about 16 golf-ball-size balls and set aside. (A 2-ounce ice cream scoop works well for this.)

recipe and ingredients continue

boss veg

203

½ teaspoon ground cumin

½ teaspoon paprika

½ teaspoon ground coriander

1 (28-ounce) can crushed tomatoes (I like San Marzano)

1 tablespoon Fast 'n' Fresh Harissa (page 33; optional)

FOR SERVING

Cooked basmati rice, couscous, or hero rolls

Cilantro, torn (optional)

6. Heat about half of the olive oil in a large skillet over medium-high heat. When the oil shimmers, fry the balls, working in batches if necessary so as not to crowd the pan, until they have a nice golden color all over, 4 to 5 minutes. (Be delicate with these, as with any balls of those you love.) Add more oil to the pan as needed.

7. Set the finished balls on the prepared baking sheet.

8. Make the sauce: Heat the olive oil in a medium pot over medium-high heat. When the oil shimmers, add the onion and season with the salt and pepper. Sauté, stirring occasionally, until soft, about

2 minutes. Stir in the garlic, turmeric, cumin, paprika, and coriander and sauté, stirring, until the onions are lightly golden, 3 to 5 more minutes.

9. Stir in the crushed tomatoes and harissa (if using) and let the pot come to a rapid simmer. Reduce the heat to medium-low and simmer the sauce until thickened and ready to cling to the meatballs (though, just a reminder, you're not simmering the balls in the sauce or they'll fall apart), about 20 minutes.

10. To serve: Serve the balls sauced over rice or couscous with a sprinkle of cilantro, if desired, or tuck them into a hero.

she's
baked

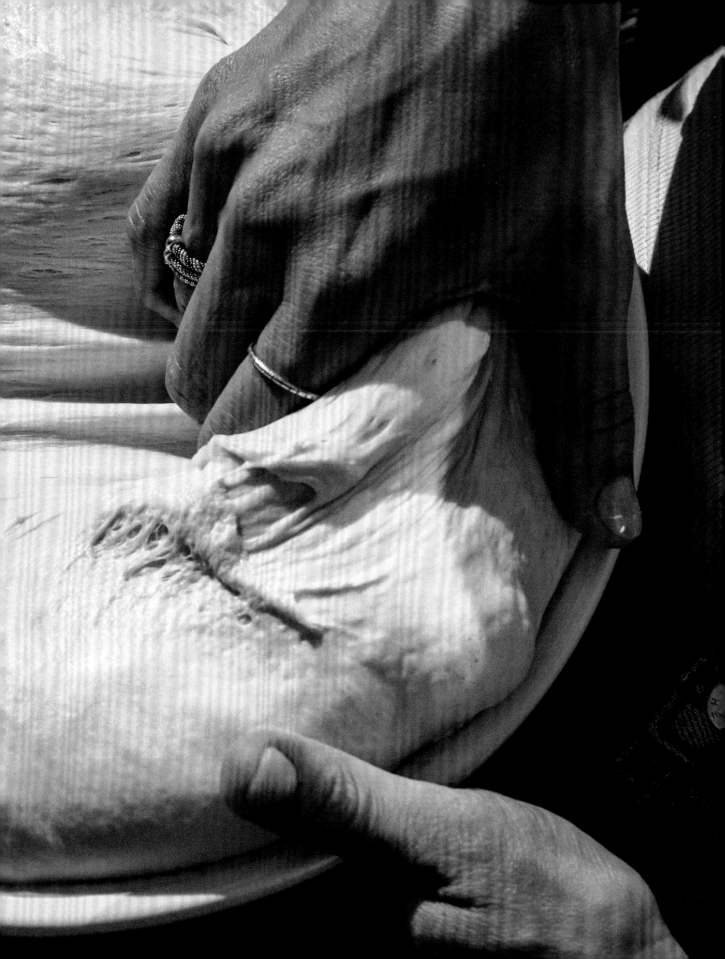

Cheekiness aside, when I think of the crowning moment of a meal, the element that brings everything together and takes a dish from "dinner" to "I am SAT. IS. FIED," I always come back to bread. Whether it's an accompaniment for **swiping and stacking**, a **vehicle for a sandwich**, or **stuffed with filling**, bread and savory baked goods are a fundamental mealtime joy. Some of my fondest memories are of walking through the Tel Aviv shuk with my dad eating a still-warm pita or Turkish boureka, or not being able to leave Jerusalem without a fresh bagel. So naturally, when I want to make a quick salad, spread, or simply prepared vegetables feel like a complete thought, I throw in **something baked and bready**—whether I'm making it from scratch or loading up something store-bought. None of these preparations require too much hands-on time, even the ones requiring you to get cozy with some dough. Honestly, I can't think of any better reason (for these recipes) to get baked right now.

corn tartines with aleppo butter and nectarines

Makes 4 tartines (serves 4)

2 large ears corn, husks and silks removed

4 tablespoons (½ stick) unsalted butter, room temperature

¾ teaspoon Aleppo pepper or red chile flakes, plus more for serving

½ teaspoon kosher salt

¼ teaspoon smoked paprika

½ cup Whipped Feta (page 82)

4 large slices sourdough bread, toasted

1 large ripe nectarine, pitted, halved, and sliced into very thin half-moons (see Note; I like a mandoline for this)

¼ cup fresh basil leaves

Flaky sea salt, for serving

Lemon wedges, for serving

Note: If your nectarine isn't as sweet and juicy as you like, you can add a drizzle of honey to finish the tartines.

When summer corn is at its juiciest and sweetest, I can't get enough of it—tossed into salads, folded into dips, gnawed straight off the cob—but I always wondered what would happen if it were heaped on top of bread. I don't know what took me so long to make my tartine dreams come true, but I finally threw caution to the wind, sautéed up a bunch of corn in a slightly obscene amount of smoky paprika-Aleppo butter, and piled it high on whipped feta-schmeared sourdough along with summer besties nectarine and basil. If that sentence didn't take your breath away, this tartine certainly will.

1. Set one ear of corn vertically in the center of a large bowl. Carefully run your knife down the cob to remove the kernels, keeping as many connected as you can. Repeat with the second ear of corn. Set aside.

2. In a small bowl, use a fork to work together the butter, Aleppo, salt, and paprika.

3. Melt the butter mixture in a large skillet over medium heat. When the butter just begins to foam, add the corn and sauté, stirring occasionally, until bright yellow and tender, about 2 minutes. Remove the pan from the heat.

4. Spread the whipped feta generously over each slice of bread. Top with the corn and a drizzle of the Aleppo butter. Lay the nectarine slices over the top and finish with the basil, a pinch of Aleppo and flaky salt, and a spritz of lemon juice.

green olive and zhoug cheesy toast

4 large slices sourdough, white bread, or Challah (page 228), or 2 Jerusalem Bagel Dinner Rolls, sliced (page 232)

1 cup Celery Zhoug (page 30)

4 slices fresh mozzarella

4 slices Gouda

½ cup Castelvetrano olives, pitted and halved

2 tablespoons unsalted butter

The thing with toast in Israel is that it's not the open-faced buttered or jammed situation we think of in North America. Rather, toasts—or toastim—are pressed grilled cheese sandwiches, ideally eaten at the beach, and always part of my must-have quick-meal rotation. I wanted to come up with a version that offered a little more wow factor, so I added tart green olives and spicy zhoug to cut through the richness of all that gooey, stringy mozzarella and make it all that much easier to inhale. Upgrade, yes, but still all those good ol' down 'n' dirty grilled cheese vibes.

1. Spread each slice of bread with the zhoug. On two slices of the bread, layer 2 slices of the mozzarella and 2 slices of the Gouda, followed by the olives. Top each with a second slice of bread, zhoug side down.

2. Butter a panini press or melt the butter in a large skillet over medium-low heat.

3. If making in a press: Carefully transfer the sandwiches to the panini press and toast until the bread is golden and the cheese is completely melted, 2 to 4 minutes.

4. If making in a skillet: Carefully transfer the sandwiches to the pan and use a spatula to press the sandwiches (a lid for a medium pot can also work) until golden on the first side, about 2 minutes. Flip the sandwiches and repeat on the other side until the cheese has completely melted, about 2 more minutes.

5. Slice in half and serve hot.

tunisian chickpea sandwich with all the fixings

Makes 2 large sandwiches (serves 2 to 4)

4 large eggs

1 (15-ounce) can chickpeas, drained and rinsed

¼ cup plus 2 tablespoons extra-virgin olive oil, plus more for serving

¼ cup fresh lemon juice (about 1 large lemon)

1 tablespoon red wine vinegar

¼ cup chopped fresh parsley leaves

¼ cup capers, drained

1 small shallot, minced

Kosher salt and freshly ground black pepper to taste

¼ cup Preserved Lemon Toum (page 41)

2 large rolls (see Note), toasted and halved

2 tablespoons Fast 'n' Fresh Harissa (page 33)

2 cups baby arugula

¼ cup oil-packed Niçoise olives, pitted

¼ cup cherry tomatoes, halved

The inspiration for this sandwich is simple: a veg-ified version of a Tunisian tuna sandwich. It's not a dramatic switch-up because chunky chickpeas are textural twins with tuna (well, close enough). And after they've sopped up a caper- and parsley-stuffed red wine vin and are piled high with jammy eggs, cured olives, harissa, and lemon toum, it's pretty much "Fish who?" It's a light-feeling yet substantial sammy that only gets better as all the layers meld—perfect for packing up for a picnic.

1. Fill a medium saucepan about three-quarters full of water and bring to a rapid boil. Carefully lower the eggs into the water and boil for 7 minutes. Immediately run the eggs under cold running water until completely cool. Peel the eggs, slice, and set aside.

2. In a large bowl, combine the chickpeas with the olive oil, lemon juice, and vinegar. Mash with the back of a fork until mostly smashed, leaving some chickpeas whole. Add the parsley, capers, and shallot and mix to combine. Season to taste with salt and pepper.

3. Generously spread the toum over the bottom half of each

roll and the harissa over the top halves.

4. Over the toum, layer the arugula, chickpea mixture, and olives. Over the harissa, layer the sliced egg and cherry tomatoes seasoned with a pinch of salt and crack of pepper.

5. Drizzle olive oil over both halves of each sandwich, carefully place the top half over the bottom, and press firmly, replacing any tomatoes or egg slices that try to escape.

6. Allow the sandwiches to sit for 10 to 15 minutes for the flavors to meld, then serve.

Note: This would be great on pretty much any kind of large roll—potato, ciabatta, demi-baguette—or even just a few slices of Herby Olive Oil Challah (page 228) or your favorite bread. But what would put it over the top is a Jerusalem Bagel Dinner Roll (page 232) made with two portions of dough combined.

smoky shakshuka sandies

Makes 4 sandwiches

3 tablespoons extra-virgin
olive oil

1 small yellow onion, finely
chopped

1 teaspoon kosher salt,
plus more to taste

½ teaspoon freshly ground
black pepper, plus more to taste

1 medium garlic clove, finely
chopped

½ teaspoon smoked paprika

½ teaspoon Fast 'n' Fresh Harissa
(page 33), Aleppo pepper, or
red chile flakes (optional)

¼ teaspoon ground cumin

3 medium tomatoes on the vine,
roughly chopped

4 large eggs

4 Jerusalem Bagel Dinner Rolls
(hoagie variation, page 235)
or 4 small hoagie buns

1 cup Garlicky Tahini (page 59)

3 medium Persian cucumbers,
thinly sliced lengthwise

3 medium radishes, thinly sliced

⅓ cup packed fresh flat-leaf
parsley leaves

When Ido was a teenager, he'd frequently stop on his way to school to get what can only be described as a vegetarian Israeli sloppy Joe. It was essentially a huge hoagie stuffed with shakshuka, or eggs simmered in a rich, thick, spiced tomato sauce. And ever since we met, he would tell me about this sandwich with so much love and affection that I had to figure out how to re-create it. I've made it a *little* bit daintier by serving it in a more manageably sized Jerusalem-style dinner roll and like to balance the richness with crisp radishes and fresh herbs, but otherwise it's stayed very true to the beloved original.

1. Heat the olive oil in a large skillet with a fitted lid over medium heat. When the oil shimmers, add the onion and season with the salt and pepper. Sauté, stirring occasionally, until translucent, about 5 minutes. Add the garlic, paprika, harissa (if using), and cumin and sauté until fragrant and the flavors have melded, 1 to 2 minutes.

2. Stir in the tomatoes and cover. Reduce the heat to medium-low and simmer until the tomatoes break down into a chunky sauce, 10 to 15 minutes. Remove the lid, season with more salt and pepper if needed, and continue simmering until the sauce is nice and jammy and thick enough to cling to the eggs, about 10 minutes.

3. Crack the eggs into the sauce, season the tops with a little salt and pepper, and cover. Increase the heat to high and cook until the whites are set but the yolks are still runny, 3 to 4 minutes. Remove the pan from the heat.

4. Slice the rolls three-quarters of the way through so they open like a book. Spread the tomato sauce over the bottom and lay an egg on top. Drizzle with tahini and layer with the cucumber and radish slices and parsley. Close 'em up and get messy.

turkish boureka three ways

The only way to describe a boureka is to have you imagine the doughiest, flakiest, crunchiest phyllo or puff pastry dough wrapped around a delicious savory filling. For me, the best-ever bourekas that I've been enjoying since I was a babe and make the first order of business to eat whenever I'm in Tel Aviv are the ones on offer at the Shuk HaCarmel at my favorite spot, called Original Turkish Bourekas. They tuck things like Bulgarian cheese or potatoes into their impossibly thin handmade phyllo dough; drench the whole thing in oil; curl it into an impressive-looking coil; bake it; and serve it with pickles, hard-boiled egg, and grated tomato for dunking. (Though my move is to get it with hot sauce and *suuuper*-sweet lemonade.) It's the perfect example of something that is both incredibly simple and yet so much more than the sum of its parts. Don't be turned off by working with the phyllo—we're using store-bought (obviously), and you can use the leftovers to make more than one of these variations (labaneh feta, masala-spiced potato, or roasted eggplant and feta) or to make Portokalopita (page 290), literally *the* perfect way to use up all the broken pieces that you think are done but don't need to be.

It's always an event when you bring these out at parties or serve them on their own as a meal, maybe with a simple salad or side veg and your favorite condiments, and let everyone have at it.

recipes continue

masala potato boureka

eggplant and feta boureka

labaneh feta boureka

labaneh feta boureka

**MAKES ONE 9-INCH BOUREKA OR 4 SMALL BOUREKAS
(SERVES 4 TO 6)**

2 cups crumbled sheep's milk feta

½ cup whole-milk ricotta,
strained in a fine-mesh sieve

⅓ cup Labaneh (page 42) or
full-fat Greek yogurt

2 large eggs

12 (16 × 13-inch) sheets phyllo
dough, thawed

⅓ cup extra-virgin olive oil

2 tablespoons sesame seeds

Celery Zhoug (page 30), for serving

Fast 'n' Fresh Harissa (page 33),
for serving

Grated Tomato for Everything
(page 38), for serving

Israeli Pickles (page 37) or
store-bought, for serving

1. Preheat the oven to 350°F.
If you are making one large
boureka, line a 9-inch round
cake pan with parchment
paper. If you are making
smaller bourekas, line two
baking sheets with parchment
paper.

2. In a medium bowl, use a
spoon to cream together the
feta, ricotta, labaneh, and one
of the eggs.

3. On a clean work surface, lay
one sheet of the phyllo so one
of the long edges is closest to
you. Brush the top with olive
oil, then layer over a second
piece. Brush with olive oil, then
layer over a third piece.

4. Spread ⅓ to ½ cup of the
cheese mixture evenly along
the bottom (long) edge of
the phyllo. Starting from the
bottom edge, roll up the filling
into the phyllo to create a
long log.

5. Repeat this process three
more times so you have a total
of four logs.

6. If making one large boureka:
Wrap the first log around the
inside edge of the pan, really
tucking in the edge of the
rolled phyllo so the log doesn't
open. Add the second piece so
the end overlaps the first by
about ½ inch, gently press the
edges together, and repeat with
the remaining logs.

7. If making smaller bourekas: Carefully bend each log into a coil. It may break in places, but that's okay! Transfer the coils to the prepared baking sheets.

8. For both versions: In a small bowl, use a fork to beat the remaining egg with 1 tablespoon of water. Brush the top of the boureka(s) with the egg wash and sprinkle with the sesame seeds. Bake for 45 to 55 minutes for a large boureka, 35 to 45 minutes for smaller ones, until the phyllo is golden brown.

9. Immediately transfer the boureka(s) to a cooling rack so the bottom and edges stay crispy and crunchy.

10. Serve hot with zhoug, harissa, grated tomato, and pickles.

masala potato boureka

MAKES ONE 9-INCH BOUREKA OR 4 SMALL BOUREKAS (SERVES 4 TO 6)

3 medium Yukon Gold potatoes, peeled, halved, then cut into thirds

3½ teaspoons kosher salt, plus more to taste

⅓ cup refined avocado or grapeseed oil

2 tablespoons black mustard seeds

2 teaspoons cumin seeds, plus more for finishing

1 large yellow onion, finely chopped

½ teaspoon freshly ground black pepper

2 medium garlic cloves, finely chopped

1 tablespoon grated fresh ginger

2 teaspoons curry powder

1 teaspoon ground turmeric

Juice of 1 lime

12 (16 × 13-inch) sheets phyllo dough, thawed

⅓ cup extra-virgin olive oil

1 large egg

Celery Zhoug (page 30), for serving

Grated Tomato for Everything (page 38), for serving

1. Preheat the oven to 350°F. If making one large boureka, line a 9-inch round cake pan with parchment paper. If making smaller bourekas, line two baking sheets with parchment paper.

recipes continue

she's baked

2. Place the potatoes in a medium pot and add just enough cold water to cover by about 1 inch. Add 1 teaspoon of the salt, bring to a boil over medium-high heat, and boil until tender, about 15 minutes. Drain and set aside to steam dry.

3. While the potatoes cook, heat the avocado oil in a large pan over medium heat. When the oil shimmers, add the mustard and cumin seeds and toast until the mustard seeds begin to pop, about 30 seconds.

4. Add the onion and season with 2 teaspoons of the salt and the pepper. Sauté, stirring occasionally, until the onions begin to caramelize, about 15 minutes. Stir in the garlic, ginger, curry powder, and turmeric and cook, stirring, until the spices begin to stick to the bottom of the pan, another 10 minutes. Add 2 tablespoons of water to the pan and use your spoon to scrape up any browned bits.

5. Cook until the onion is fully caramelized, about 5 more minutes, stirring frequently to keep the onion from burning. Stir in the lime juice and remove the pan from the heat. Add the cooked potatoes and season with the remaining ½ teaspoon salt, mixing until everything is well coated in the spices. Taste and season with more salt, if needed. Set aside.

6. On a clean work surface, lay one sheet of the phyllo so one of the long edges is closest to you. Brush the top with olive oil, then layer over a second piece. Brush with olive oil, then layer over a third piece.

7. Spread ¾ cup of the potato mixture evenly along the bottom (long) edge of the phyllo. Starting from the bottom edge, roll up the filling into the phyllo to create a long log.

8. Repeat this process three more times so you have a total of four logs.

9. If making one large boureka: Wrap the first log around the inside edge of the pan, really tucking in the edge of the rolled phyllo so the log doesn't open. Add the second piece so the end overlaps the first by about ½ inch, gently press the edges together, and repeat with the remaining logs.

10. **If making smaller bourekas:** Carefully bend each log into a coil. It may break in places, but that's okay! Transfer the coils to the prepared baking sheets.

11. **For both versions:** In a small bowl, use a fork to beat the egg with 1 tablespoon of water. Brush the top of the boureka(s) with the egg wash and sprinkle with cumin seeds. Bake for 45 to 55 minutes for a large boureka, 35 to 45 minutes for smaller ones, until the phyllo is golden brown.

12. Immediately transfer the boureka(s) to a cooling rack so the bottom and edges stay crispy and crunchy.

13. Serve hot with zhoug and grated tomato.

eggplant and feta boureka

MAKES ONE 9-INCH BOUREKA OR 4 SMALL BOUREKAS (SERVES 4 TO 6)

¼ cup extra-virgin olive oil, plus ⅓ cup for brushing the dough

1 large eggplant, peeled and cut into ½-inch chunks

1 teaspoon kosher salt

12 (16 × 13-inch) sheets phyllo dough, thawed

1⅓ cups crumbled sheep's milk feta

1 large egg

2 tablespoons nigella or sesame seeds

Celery Zhoug (page 30), for serving

Grated Tomato for Everything (page 38), for serving

1. Heat ¼ cup of the olive oil in a large skillet over medium heat. When the oil shimmers, add the eggplant, toss to coat in the oil, and season with the salt. Reduce the heat to medium-low and sauté, stirring occasionally, until the eggplant is golden, 20 to 25 minutes. Remove from the heat.

2. Preheat the oven to 350°F. If making one large boureka, line a 9-inch round cake pan with parchment paper. If making smaller bourekas, line two baking sheets with parchment paper.

3. On a clean work surface, lay one sheet of the phyllo so one of the long edges is closest to you. Brush the top with olive

recipe continues

oil, then layer over a second piece. Brush with olive oil, then layer over a third piece.

4. Spread a quarter of the eggplant mixture evenly along the bottom (long) edge of the phyllo and top with a quarter of the feta. Starting from the bottom edge, roll up the filling into the phyllo to create a long log.

5. Repeat this process three more times so you have a total of four logs.

6. If making one large boureka: Wrap the first log around the inside edge of the pan, really tucking in the edge of the rolled phyllo so the log doesn't open. Add the second piece so the end overlaps the first by about ½ inch, gently press the edges together, and repeat with the remaining logs.

7. If making smaller bourekas: Carefully bend each log into a coil. It may break in places, but that's okay! Transfer the coils to the prepared baking sheets.

8. For both versions: In a small bowl, use a fork to beat the egg with 1 tablespoon of water. Brush the top of the boureka(s) with the egg wash and sprinkle with the nigella seeds. Bake for 45 to 55 minutes for a large boureka, 35 to 45 minutes for smaller ones, until the phyllo is golden brown.

9. Immediately transfer the boureka(s) to a cooling rack so the bottom and edges stay crispy and crunchy.

10. Serve hot with zhoug and grated tomato.

challah khachapuri with eggs, herbs, and all the cheese

2 cups grated low-moisture mozzarella

¾ cup crumbled sheep's milk feta

¾ cup whole-milk ricotta

¼ cup finely chopped fresh flat-leaf parsley, plus more for serving

1 large egg plus 3 large egg yolks

2 medium garlic cloves, minced

½ teaspoon kosher salt

½ teaspoon freshly ground black pepper

½ recipe Herby Olive Oil Challah dough (page 228), proofed once

All-purpose flour, for dusting

Nigella seeds and/or sesame seeds, for sprinkling

Sumac, for serving

Celery Zhoug (page 30), for serving

The Shuk HaCarmel is the largest open-air market in Tel Aviv, and it really is the crown jewel of the city. You could spend an entire day strolling through rows upon rows of vendors selling the freshest spices, produce, meats, and prepared foods and eat very, very well while doing so. It's also the perfect representation of all the cultural flavors that make up the Israeli culinary voice—there's fresh Druze pita; Yemeni jachnun; and, my new personal favorite, Georgian khachapuri. It's like a dough "boat" that's been stuffed with a tangy, melty mix of cheeses and topped with a runny egg, all of which you can swab and scoop with the soft bready edges—which I just so happen to make with the leftover half of herby challah dough. Drizzled with zhoug, it's the ultimate comfort food.

1. In a medium bowl, combine the mozzarella, feta, ricotta, parsley, whole egg, garlic, salt, and pepper. Stir to thoroughly mix and set aside.

2. Line a baking sheet with parchment paper.

3. Divide the prepared dough into two equal halves. Lightly flour a work surface, then use a rolling pin to roll each half into a ¼-inch-thick circle 10 to 12 inches in diameter. You can also use your hands to help pull the dough into this shape.

4. Tightly roll up two opposite sides of the dough to create an oblong "boat" that's about 4 inches wide at its widest point. Pinch the ends together and give them a twist to tightly seal.

5. Carefully transfer both pieces of dough to the prepared baking sheet. Divide the filling between the two khachapuri, spreading it evenly over the center. Cover the khachapuri with a towel and allow them to

recipe continues

she's baked

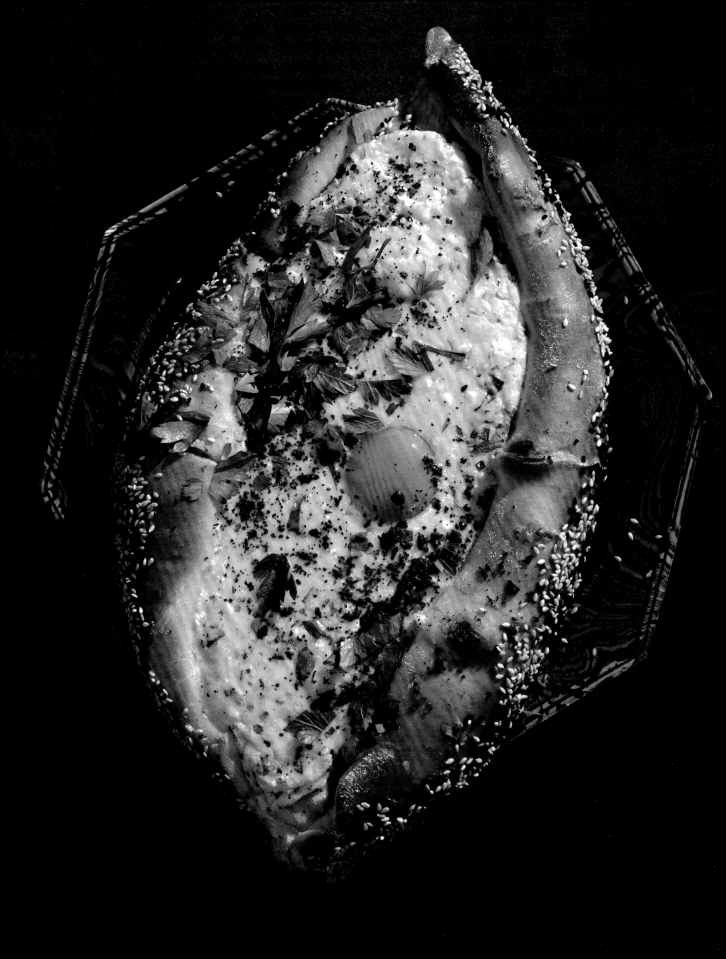

proof until the oven is heated, about 15 minutes.

6. Preheat the oven to 450°F.

7. In a small bowl, use a fork to beat one of the egg yolks with 1 tablespoon of water and brush the egg wash over the khachapuri crusts in a thick layer. Sprinkle with the nigella and/or sesame seeds and bake for about 15 minutes, until the crust begins to lightly brown and the cheese is melted.

8. Remove the baking sheet from the oven and gently press the back of a spoon into the middle of the filling of both khachapuri to make a small well. Add one egg yolk to each.

9. Return the baking sheet to the oven and cook until the yolks are warmed through but runny, about 3 minutes.

10. Top each khachapuri with a sprinkle of sumac and parsley and serve immediately with zhoug.

11. To dig in, break off one end of the khachapuri and use it to stir the runny egg into the cheese. Continue to rip more pieces off the bread boat to dip into the filling while it's still hot.

herby olive oil challah

1¼ cups warm water (105–110°F)

4 teaspoons active dry yeast

½ cup sugar, plus a pinch

5¾ to 6 cups all-purpose flour

3 large eggs plus 2 large egg yolks

⅓ cup extra-virgin olive oil, plus more as needed

2 tablespoons kosher salt

6 to 8 small fresh sage sprigs

6 to 8 small fresh oregano sprigs

Flaky sea salt to taste

I feel like it's finally time to combine my two greatest loves: fresh herbs and challah. After all, I couldn't write this book—or any book—and not include a challah. Aside from having a sacred place in my family's traditions, it's also the ultimate blank canvas (and just really effing good bread, plus also incredibly easy to make and hard to fuck up). First, I swapped out the neutral oil you usually use when making this bread for a fruity olive oil to lend beautiful depth and richness. But the real showstopping moment is braiding sprigs of sage and oregano right into the dough. It not only looks like you've been making artisanal loaves in your gorgeous country kitchen your whole life, but it also perfumes the bread with a subtle herbaceous flavor. This is one seriously special challah.

1. In a medium bowl, combine the water and yeast with a pinch of sugar. Let the mixture sit for 5 minutes to activate the yeast, which should start to get foamy.

2. In the bowl of a stand mixer fitted with the dough hook, combine 5¾ cups of the flour, the sugar, whole eggs, one of the egg yolks, and the olive oil. Add the yeast mixture and mix on medium speed just until the dough comes together. Sprinkle in the salt and mix on medium speed until the dough pulls away from the sides of the bowl and is smooth, about 5 minutes. If the dough is still pretty sticky at this point, add the remaining ¼ cup flour and mix until smooth.

3. Turn out the dough onto a clean work surface and knead until it is soft and smooth, about 2 minutes. Return the dough to the mixer bowl, cover the bowl with a damp towel, and allow the dough to rise in a warm place until doubled in size, 1 to 1½ hours.

recipe continues

Note: The fresh herb possibilities for this challah are endless—try it with chives, chive blossoms, thyme, rosemary, or any combination.

4. Line two baking sheets with parchment paper or silicone baking mats. Remove the dough from the bowl and divide it into two even pieces. Keep one piece under a towel while you braid the other.

5. Divide the piece of dough you're working with into three even pieces. Roll out each into a nice long rope, 1 to 1½ inches thick. Place the strands parallel on one of the prepared baking sheets, about 1 inch apart. Gather up the ends of one side of the strands and gently press them together—this will hold your challah together as you braid. Begin braiding by lifting the piece on the right and passing it over the center strand (so that it is now in the center). Take the strand on the left and bring it to the center. Continue in this pattern—outside to center—trying to keep the braid as tight as possible and tucking in sprigs of herbs as you go so it looks as though they're braided into the dough. When you've gotten to the bottom of the ropes, pinch the ends together and

gently tuck them under the loaf. Transfer the dough to a prepared baking sheet.

6. Cover with a damp towel while you repeat with the second half of the dough. Cover both loaves with the towel and let them rise in a warm place for 1 hour.

7. Preheat the oven to 350°F.

8. In a small bowl, use a fork to beat the remaining egg yolk with 1 tablespoon of water. Brush the egg wash over the two loaves and brush the herbs with olive oil. Sprinkle with flaky salt and bake for 35 to 45 minutes, until golden and fluffy. Let cool before slicing—but also, so nice to eat when still a bit warm.

9. Store the challah in beeswax wrap or a zip-top bag at room temperature for up to 5 days. After a couple days it will start to dry out, but that just means challah French toast is in your future.

jerusalem bagel dinner rolls and bagels

Makes 8 rolls or bagels

¾ cup warm water (105–110°F)

2 teaspoons active dry yeast

3 tablespoons sugar, plus a pinch

2½ cups all-purpose flour, plus more for dusting

2 tablespoons refined avocado or grapeseed oil

2 tablespoons whole milk

2 tablespoons full-fat Greek yogurt

1½ teaspoons kosher salt

1 cup ice water

1½ cups sesame seeds

Flaky sea salt to taste

Note: You could also shape the dough into four equal portions and roll it into longer hoagie rolls (see the variation on page 235), which are perfect for the Smoky Shakshuka Sandies (page 217) and Tunisian Chickpea Sandwich with All the Fixings (page 214). Your bake time will increase slightly.

There is not a trip to Israel where I don't make a point of visiting the Jerusalem markets and buying a toasty-sweet, sesame-coated bagel that's hopefully straight from the oven and still way too hot to comfortably hold but I do it anyway since that's just the game because when they are fresh, it truly feels like you just won the lottery. Unlike most bagels outside the Levant, Jerusalem bagels, or ka'ak al Quds, as they're called in Arabic (literally "Jerusalem bread"), aren't boiled, so they're more tender and fluffy than dense and chewy. Since I didn't want to have to wait until I got back to Israel to have that pain-as-pleasure moment, I figured out how to make them in my own oven but with more shape variations so they work with a wider variety of dishes. This recipe takes that same sesame-studded goodness but delivers it in dinner roll form so you can offer up a pile of them for everyone to tear and dunk accordingly. That said, you can also shape these into the more traditional oval with a hole in the center.

1. In a medium bowl, combine the warm water and yeast with a pinch of sugar. Let the mixture sit for 5 minutes to activate the yeast, which should start to get foamy.

2. In the bowl of a stand mixer fitted with the dough hook, combine the flour, sugar, avocado oil, milk, and yogurt. Add the yeast mixture and mix on medium speed just to combine. Add the salt and mix again on medium speed until the dough is sticky but smooth, 15 minutes. Cover the bowl with a damp towel and allow the dough to rise in a warm place until doubled in size, 1 to 1½ hours.

recipe continues

tahini baby

232

3. Line a baking sheet with parchment paper.

4. Punch down the dough and turn it out onto a lightly floured work surface. Divide the dough into eight even pieces and cover them with a towel.

5. If making dinner rolls: Gently flatten the first piece of dough with the heel of your hand, then tuck the edges up and into the center of the dough so they meet in the middle and form a tight round shape. Turn the dough over and shape into a ball by gently holding the dough between your thumb and fingers while keeping the edge of your hand on the counter (instead of pressing down on the dough from above with your palm).

6. Using your fingers, carefully roll two sides of each ball, about ½ inch on either side, to create a little football shape. Pinch the ends. Arrange the finished dough balls on the prepared baking sheet and cover with a towel.

7. If making bagels: Shape the dough into balls as described above. Then use your finger to make a hole in the center of each ball and use your hands to gently stretch the hole until it is about 2 inches wide. From here you could either go for a round shape or a more traditional oval. Arrange the bagels on the prepared baking sheet and cover with a towel.

8. Fill a medium bowl with the ice water. Place the sesame seeds in another medium bowl.

9. Dip each roll or bagel into the water, then into the sesame seeds, making sure to completely cover the dough. Place the coated dough back onto the baking sheet and immediately sprinkle with flaky salt. Cover with a damp towel and allow the dough to proof in a warm place until fluffy, 45 minutes to 1 hour.

10. Preheat the oven to 425°F. Line a large bowl with a towel.

11. Bake the rolls or bagels for 10 minutes. Spray the dough with water or use your hand to flick water at it (which is lazy girl approved and what I do). Bake until the bread is lightly golden all over and sounds hollow when you tap the bottom, about 3 more minutes.

12. Place the rolls or bagels in the prepared bowl and cover with another towel for 5 to 10 minutes. The steam will keep them fluffy while you finish with the remaining dough.

13. When cooled, store in an airtight container at room temperature for up to 3 days. To revive slightly stale rolls, give them a sprinkle of water and toast them in the oven until warmed through.

VARIATION:

jerusalem hoagies

If you want a bigger sandwich roll (which would be perfect for the Smoky Shakshuka Sandies on page 217), you can combine two pieces of dough and shape one large roll. You may need to add up to 5 minutes of bake time.

laffa two ways

Laffa is a soft, super-chewy Iraqi flatbread, and most of the best meals of my life have involved using laffa to bundle up some variation of kebabs, shawarma, and salatim. In restaurants they are often so large that when they come out in a big basket, they take up at least a third of the table, and everyone risks burning their hands in order to tear off the doughiest, freshest pieces possible. Even though you probably don't have a taboon, or clay oven, at home, you can still make a super-tasty homemade laffa by using your grill or a pan (or oven, if you're slathering these in za'atar oil). The prep and hands-on time is minimal, and the reward is a stack of fluffy, piping-hot laffa you can serve up with all the things.

sesame laffa

MAKES 8 LAFFA

2 cups warm water (105–110°F)

1 tablespoon active dry yeast

2 tablespoons sugar, plus a pinch

4¾ cups all-purpose flour, plus more as needed

¼ cup extra-virgin olive oil

2½ teaspoons kosher salt

Refined avocado or grapeseed oil, for greasing

½ medium or large onion (if grilling)

½ cup sesame seeds (optional; see Note, page 238)

1. In the bowl of a stand mixer fitted with the dough hook, combine the water and yeast with a pinch of sugar. Let the mixture sit for 5 minutes to activate the yeast, which should start to get foamy.

2. Add the sugar, flour, and olive oil and mix on medium–low speed just to combine. When the dough comes together, sprinkle in the salt and knead on

recipes continue

Note: Feel free to omit the sesame seeds and make these plain.

medium-low speed until the dough is smooth and slightly tacky, 10 minutes. It shouldn't gob onto your fingers; if it does, add up to 1½ tablespoons of flour, 1 teaspoon at a time, until it's where you need it to be.

3. Lightly grease a large bowl with avocado oil. Place the dough in the bowl and cover with a damp towel. Allow the dough to rise in a warm place until doubled in size, 1 to 1½ hours.

4. Line a baking sheet with parchment paper or a silicone baking mat.

5. Punch down the dough and turn it out onto a clean work surface lightly dusted with flour. Cut the dough into eight equal pieces and roll them into balls. Arrange them on the baking sheet, keeping at least a couple inches between each. Cover the dough with a damp towel and allow the dough to proof in a warm place until doubled in size, 30 to 45 minutes.

6. If grilling: Heat a grill to medium-high heat. Clean the grill with a grill brush and use the halved onion to coat the grates with oil.

7. If making on the stove: Soak a paper towel with oil and use it to lightly coat a large cast-iron pan. Don't throw away the paper towel; you'll need it every time you place down a fresh laffa. Heat the pan over medium-high heat.

8. For both methods: Lightly flour a clean work surface and sprinkle with about 1 tablespoon of the sesame seeds (if using). Take out each ball of dough and use a rolling pin to roll out the dough into a ⅛-inch-thick circle (about 9 inches wide). You'll want to add more flour and sesame seeds between each ball of dough.

9. Place the dough on the grill or in the skillet and cook until the top is bubbling and there are some golden spots on the bottom, 50 seconds to 1 minute. Flip and cook on the other side until it's also golden in spots. Repeat with the other balls of dough.

10. Eat immediately, or wrap in a clean towel to keep soft and warm.

recipes continue

za'atar laffa

MAKES 8 LAFFA

1 cup Za'atar (page 25)

1 cup extra-virgin olive oil

1 recipe Sesame Laffa (page 236), proofed but not yet rolled with sesame seeds

Flaky sea salt to taste

1. Position an oven rack in the middle of the oven and place a pizza stone or overturned baking sheet on top. Preheat the oven to 500°F. Prepare eight squares of parchment paper, about 12 × 12 inches each.

2. In a medium bowl, stir together the za'atar and olive oil. Set aside.

3. When ready to bake, lightly flour a clean work surface. Take out each ball of dough and dust it with flour. Use a rolling pin to roll out the dough into a ⅛-inch-thick circle (about 9 inches wide).

4. Set the rolled-out dough onto a piece of parchment paper and drizzle each circle with 2½ tablespoons of the za'atar oil. Use a spatula or the back of a spoon to spread the oil evenly over the surface and sprinkle generously with flaky salt.

5. Carefully transfer the parchment and dough to the pizza stone—you will need to do this in batches—and bake for 5 minutes, until fluffy and golden in spots. Carefully remove the laffa, peel off the parchment, and eat hot with everything in this book.

grains
on grains
on pasta
(and legumes)

Grains and legumes are the backbones of Middle Eastern cooking. But while these ingredients are hearty and substantial—and yes, rice and beans are the main sources of protein in a plant-forward diet—their applications go well beyond the one-note, utilitarian dishes that people assume come with being vegetarian. We're talking **nut- and dried fruit–studded, spice-infused, herb-confetti'd, brothy, saucy next-level magic**. They also check every box for me when it comes to making no-fuss meals—they're quick cooking, inexpensive, and belly filling. These recipes will always have a spot on my table, whether they're complementing another dish in this book or having their own special moment for a **simple but deeply satisfying** meal.

caramelized onion and noodle pilaf

Serves 4

3 tablespoons unsalted butter

2 tablespoons extra-virgin olive oil

1 large yellow onion, finely diced

1 cup vermicelli noodles, broken into 1-inch pieces

2 cups basmati rice, rinsed until the water runs clear

1½ teaspoons kosher salt

¼ teaspoon ground cinnamon

¼ teaspoon allspice

Freshly ground black pepper to taste

I've had this traditional Lebanese dish many times over the years, and each time I'm mesmerized by the texture of toasted vermicelli noodles scattered among the rice. It's a cozy, comforting side yet elevated thanks to heady cinnamon and allspice and succulent caramelized onions. You could keep this in the fridge to graze on, use it as the base of a grain bowl, or serve it as a flavor-enhancing side.

1. In a medium pot, heat the butter and olive oil over medium heat. When the butter is melted, add the onion and cook, stirring occasionally, until deeply golden, about 15 minutes. Transfer the onion to a small bowl and set aside.

2. Add the noodles and toast, stirring occasionally, until browned—taking care not to burn them—about 2 minutes. Stir in the rice and caramelized onion and season with the salt, cinnamon, allspice, and a few cracks of pepper. Add 3 cups of water, stir, and cover the pot. Allow the mixture to come to a boil, then reduce the heat to a simmer. Cook until all the water has evaporated, 10 to 12 minutes.

3. Turn off the heat and keep covered to steam for at least 10 minutes. When ready to serve, fluff the rice and noodles with a fork and season with more salt and pepper if needed.

4. Store leftovers in a sealed container in the fridge for up to 3 days.

spicy green rice with dukkah

Serves 4

¾ cup packed fresh baby spinach

½ cup packed fresh cilantro leaves, plus more for serving

½ cup packed fresh mint leaves

½ cup packed fresh chives

1 medium serrano chile, jalapeño, or long-hot chile, stemmed (seeds removed if you want less heat, or omit entirely)

2 medium garlic cloves, peeled

¼ cup extra-virgin olive oil, plus more for serving

1½ cups basmati rice, rinsed until the water runs clear

1½ teaspoons kosher salt

Juice of ½ lemon

1½ cups Fennel Seed Pistachio Dukkah (page 92)

Labaneh (page 42) or plain yogurt, for serving (optional)

A couple summers ago I was having lunch at a cute little café in Tel Aviv, where they had this brilliantly emerald-green herbed rice, and I could not get out of my head how much fresh lift and complexity the herbs gave the otherwise simple dish. I wanted to take that factor way (way) over the top and came up with this version, which blends earthy-sweet spinach with cilantro, mint, chives, and jalapeños plus punchy garlic and a sprinkle of fennel-y pistachio dukkah—kinda like an arroz verde with Middle Eastern flair.

1. In a high-speed blender or food processor, combine the spinach, cilantro, mint, chives, chile (if using), and garlic with ½ cup of water. Blend until smooth and bright green. Transfer the sauce to a large measuring cup and add enough water so that the mixture totals 3 cups. Set aside.

2. Heat the olive oil in a medium pot over medium heat. When the oil shimmers, add the rice and toast until just translucent and fragrant, about 5 minutes. Season with the salt and pour in the sauce and water mixture. Increase the heat to medium-high and allow the pot to come to a boil, then reduce to a simmer. Cover and allow the rice to steam for 10 minutes.

3. Turn off the heat but keep the pot covered to steam the rice for another 10 minutes. Sprinkle the rice with the lemon juice, season with more salt if needed, and fluff with a fork.

4. To serve, spread the rice over a shallow serving bowl and scatter the dukkah over the top. Finish with cilantro and a drizzle of olive oil. Serve with labaneh or yogurt, if desired.

5. Store leftovers in a sealed container in the fridge for up to 3 days.

hawaij "chicken" soup

¼ cup plus 2 tablespoons extra-virgin olive oil, plus more as needed

4 large carrots, chopped into 1-inch pieces

1 large parsnip, peeled and cut into 1-inch pieces

1 medium leek, ends trimmed, dark green leaves removed, halved vertically and rinsed then sliced into 1-inch-thick half-moons

2 large yellow onions, quartered

1 head garlic, halved widthwise

1 tablespoon garlic powder

1 tablespoon dried fenugreek leaves (see Note)

2 teaspoons Savory Hawaij (page 24) or curry powder

1 teaspoon ground turmeric

2 tablespoons kosher salt, plus more to taste

1 teaspoon freshly ground black pepper, plus more to taste

6 celery stalks with leaves, chopped into 1-inch pieces

2 large Yukon Gold potatoes, peeled and quartered

1 (2 × 3-inch) Parmesan rind (optional; see Note, page 252)

1 cup packed fresh flat-leaf parsley leaves

I will tell anyone visiting Israel that their must-do list has to include a trip to the Yemenite Quarter in Tel Aviv. I grew up eating my way through the family-run restaurants there, which offer a handful of rustic dishes and stews ladled from huge pots simmering away on the stove. They are straightforward meals, but there is nothing simple about their layers of deep, rich flavor. I wanted to create that same cozy, savory deep dive with this soup, which in spirit is the classic matzo ball soup you know and love but with the added interest of Yemeni hawaij. It's the perfect cook-once-eat-all-week soup or special Friday night dish with herby matzo balls, and not once will you miss the chicken.

1. Heat 2 tablespoons of the olive oil in a large stockpot over medium-high heat. When the oil shimmers, add about half of the carrots, parsnip, and leek. Sauté, stirring occasionally, until they just begin to caramelize, about 7 minutes. Transfer the mixture to a medium bowl and repeat with the second half of the vegetables, adding more oil to the pot if needed. Transfer the cooked veggies to the bowl and set aside.

2. Heat the remaining ¼ cup olive oil in the same pot over medium-high heat. When the oil shimmers, add the onions and head of garlic and sauté, stirring occasionally, until lightly charred on the edges, about 4 minutes. Stir in the garlic powder, fenugreek, hawaij, and turmeric and cook until the spices release their aromas, about 1 minute. Season with the salt and pepper.

3. Add 4½ quarts of water to the pot along with the sautéed vegetables, celery, potatoes, and Parm rind (if using). Bring the pot to a boil over medium-

recipe and ingredients continue

1 (15-ounce) can chickpeas, drained and rinsed

Steamed basmati rice or Herby Matzo Balls (recipe follows), for serving (optional)

Lemon wedges, for serving (optional)

high heat, then reduce to a simmer. Allow the soup to simmer for 45 minutes.

4. Add the parsley and chickpeas and simmer until the chickpeas are soft but not falling apart and the broth is reduced and more concentrated in flavor, 15 to 20 minutes. Season with more salt and pepper, if needed.

5. Remove and discard the garlic, or if you like the idea of big sweet-hot garlicky bites, remove the cloves from the skin and add them back to the pot.

6. Serve the soup on its own with steamed rice or with herby matzo balls, along with lemon wedges, if desired.

7. Store leftovers in a sealed container in the fridge for up to 1 week.

Note: I like to make this soup ahead and let it sit on the stove off the heat to continue to steep and develop even more flavor. Also, I love saving up the rinds from my Parmesan to toss into soups for even more body and flavor when I'm not cooking with meat. So even though I know Parm isn't exactly the most obvious choice in this dish, it does get the job done for adding even more depth of flavor. But if you don't happen to have one lying in the cheese drawer, don't worry about it. The same thing goes for fenugreek leaves—these take the flavor to the next level, so I strongly encourage you to seek them out. But if you can't find them or it's not gonna happen, skip it.

herby matzo balls

Traditional matzo balls get a mini makeover with fresh herbs (although feel free to leave out the cilantro, if that's not your thing).

MAKES 22 SMALL BALLS

2 cups matzo meal

6 large eggs

⅓ cup refined avocado or grapeseed oil

2 tablespoons finely chopped fresh cilantro leaves

1 tablespoon finely chopped fresh flat-leaf parsley leaves

1 tablespoon kosher salt, plus more to taste

1 teaspoon freshly ground black pepper, plus more for serving

1 teaspoon garlic powder

1 teaspoon onion powder

2 teaspoons baking powder

1. In a large bowl, combine the matzo meal, eggs, oil, cilantro, parsley, salt, pepper, garlic powder, onion powder, baking powder, and ½ cup of water. Stir until the mixture is well incorporated. Cover the bowl with plastic wrap and refrigerate for at least 20 minutes or up to overnight.

2. Bring a large pot of water to a boil over medium-high heat and season well with salt.

3. Using wet hands, roll the matzo mixture into golf-ball-size balls. Add the balls to the water, cover, and reduce to a simmer. Allow the matzo balls to simmer until fluffy and cooked through, 25 to 30 minutes.

4. Keep the balls in the water until ready to serve with broth, ideally finished with a couple cracks of pepper.

5. To store leftovers, remove the matzo balls from the water or broth and keep in a sealed container in the fridge for up to 3 days.

sunny cherry rice

2 cups Buttery Saffron Rice (page 265)

1½ cups cherries (sour cherries, if you can find them), pitted and halved

¾ cup slivered almonds, toasted in a dry pan until lightly golden

¼ cup fresh mint, torn

¼ cup fresh tarragon leaves, finely chopped

2 tablespoons finely chopped fresh chives

Grated zest and juice of 1 lime

2 tablespoons extra-virgin olive oil

2 teaspoons honey

Flaky sea salt, for serving

This dish is exactly what it sounds like—light and bright with big juicy chunks of fresh cherries. Because when cherry season drops, you gotta use them in anything and everything—and what could be better than a cheeky, beachy rice dish? I use my buttery saffron rice as the base—because can you even with that gorgeous golden color?—then stuff it full of fresh herbs, almonds, and, of course, cherries. She's a side; she's a main; she's a star.

1. When the rice has finished steaming, fluff it with a fork and spread it over a shallow serving plate. Scatter the top with the cherries, almonds, mint, tarragon, and chives. Sprinkle with the lime zest and juice, and drizzle with the olive oil and honey. Finish with flaky salt and serve.

2. Store in a sealed container in the fridge for up to 2 days.

harira

¼ cup extra-virgin olive oil

1 large yellow onion, finely
chopped

2 medium carrots, finely
chopped

3 celery stalks, finely chopped

Kosher salt and freshly ground
black pepper to taste

3 medium garlic cloves,
finely chopped

1 heaping tablespoon
finely grated fresh ginger
(I like a Microplane for this)

2 tablespoons Fast 'n'
Fresh Harissa (page 33),
or 2 teaspoons red chile flakes,
plus more for serving

1 teaspoon ground turmeric

1 teaspoon ground cumin

1 teaspoon ground coriander

Pinch of ground cinnamon

2 tablespoons tomato paste

1 cup French lentils, rinsed and
picked over

1 (28-ounce) can crushed
tomatoes (I like San Marzano)

1 (15-ounce) can chickpeas,
drained and rinsed

Juice of 1 lemon

Sliced lemon, for garnish

Fresh cilantro or parsley leaves,
for garnish

If there were ever a mic-drop dish to put an end to the idea that veg dishes can't fill you up, this Moroccan stew is it. It's packed with (protein-rich) lentils and chickpeas, and while it does feel light and brothy, the smoky hits you get from cumin, cinnamon, and harissa and the tomatoey body put it squarely in satisfying territory. Ladle this over rice and/or scoop it up with some good crusty bread—or just dig in as is—and call it dinner.

1. Heat the olive oil in a large pot over medium heat. When the oil shimmers, add the onion, carrots, and celery. Season with salt and pepper and sauté, stirring occasionally, until the onion is translucent, about 5 minutes. Add the garlic and ginger and cook until just fragrant, about 30 seconds.

2. Stir in the harissa, turmeric, cumin, coriander, and cinnamon and allow the mixture to toast slightly, about 30 seconds. Stir in the tomato paste and cook until it has deepened in color, 3 to 4 minutes. Add the lentils with another pinch of salt and pepper and stir to combine.

3. Stir in the crushed tomatoes with 8 cups of water and increase the heat to medium-high. When the mixture comes to a boil, cover, reduce the heat to medium, and simmer for 20 minutes.

4. Add the chickpeas, cover, and cook for another 15 minutes, until the lentils are al dente, the vegetables are tender, and the flavors have melded. Season with more salt, if needed. (Don't be shy!)

5. To serve, stir in the lemon juice and divide the soup among serving bowls. Garnish with more harissa, lemon slices, and cilantro.

the greenest falafel

¾ cup dried chickpeas, soaked overnight and drained

1 medium yellow onion, roughly chopped

1 bunch fresh cilantro, leaves and tender stems (about 1½ packed cups)

1 bunch fresh flat-leaf parsley, leaves and tender stems (about 1½ packed cups)

¼ cup fresh mint leaves

5 medium garlic cloves, peeled

1½ teaspoons kosher salt, plus more to taste

1 teaspoon baking powder

1 teaspoon ground cumin

½ teaspoon ground coriander

½ teaspoon ground cardamom

¼ cup refined avocado or grapeseed oil, plus more as needed

FOR EXTRA CREDIT

Laffa (page 236)

Garlicky Tahini (page 59)

Celery Zhoug (page 30)

Chopped Salad (see page 53)

Israeli Pickles (page 37)

My goal for this falafel—aside from making it your new go-to fluffy, crispy cloud of chickpea goodness—was that I wanted you to crack it open and be blinded by the bright green color. All those herbs stuffed into the mix are the key to keeping them light enough to pop into your regular lunch/dinner/snack rotation (and your mouth). Also, that frying them at a higher temperature means you'll nail that crunchy exterior and—as much as I don't want to say it—moist interior.

1. In a large bowl, combine the drained chickpeas with the onion, cilantro, parsley, mint, garlic, salt, baking powder, cumin, coriander, and cardamom. Working in batches, transfer the mixture to a food processor and process until evenly broken down, bright green, and just shy of super smooth. (You're not going for completely smooth.) Transfer the blended mixture to a medium bowl and repeat with the remaining mixture.

2. Shape the mixture into 1½-ounce balls (I like using a small ice cream scoop for this) and set aside. Line a large plate with paper towels.

3. Heat the oil in a large skillet over medium-high heat. When the oil shimmers, add enough of the falafel balls to the pan so they fit comfortably with some room around them. Fry until the falafel is dark golden brown on all sides, 3 to 5 minutes total. Transfer to the lined plate and immediately sprinkle with salt. Continue with the remaining falafel, adding more oil to the pan if needed.

4. For the deluxe falafel experience, layer them in a laffa and top with garlicky tahini, zhoug, chopped salad, Israeli pickles, and any of the condiments or dips in chapter 2. Or pile them on a salad, stuff them in a pita, or enjoy any way you love falafel.

egg-fried bulgur

Serves 4 to 6

1 cup whole-grain bulgur

1½ cups vegetable stock or water

2 tablespoons extra-virgin olive oil

2 teaspoons kosher salt

2 tablespoons refined avocado or grapeseed oil, plus more as needed

4 large garlic cloves, minced

½ bunch asparagus, ends trimmed and chopped into bite-size pieces

2 large eggs

1 cup fresh or frozen peas (see Note, page 262)

Juice of 1 lime

Freshly ground black pepper to taste

⅓ cup finely chopped fresh chives, plus more for serving

Garlicky Tahini (page 59), for serving

Fast 'n' Fresh Harissa (page 33), for serving

This dish exists 100 percent because of Ido, who is not only an egg-fried-rice freak but also a huge fan of bulgur, that super-nutty, super-chewy, earthy grain that's like rice plumped up on steroids. He didn't have to ask me twice to try to incorporate it into one of our Chinese take-out favorites, and believe me when I tell you that we've never looked back since. The crispy, garlicky grains get loaded up with egg and veg—which you can mix and match depending on what you have in the fridge—then drizzled with harissa and tahini. But the best part is the fact that, especially if you cook the grains in advance, you can get this on the table in minutes.

1. Rinse the bulgur under cold water and drain well. Set aside.

2. In a medium pot, bring the stock to a boil over medium-high heat. Stir in the bulgur, 1 tablespoon of the olive oil, and 1 teaspoon of the salt. Allow the pot to come back up to a boil, then reduce to a simmer and cover. Cook until the liquid has been fully absorbed and the bulgur is tender, 10 to 12 minutes.

3. Remove the pot from the heat and let it stand, covered, for another 10 minutes. Fluff with a fork and allow to cool

completely. You could also refrigerate the bulgur at this point; it will keep in a sealed container for up to 3 days.

4. Heat the avocado oil and garlic in a large skillet over medium heat. Sauté until the garlic is fragrant, 30 to 60 seconds. Add the asparagus and cook, stirring occasionally, until it softens and turns bright green, 2 to 3 minutes. Stir in the bulgur, breaking up any clumps with your spoon. Cook until it gets crisp and fragrant, about 3 minutes.

recipe continues

tahini baby

260

Note: If you happen to see fresh fava beans at the market, add a cup of them with the peas for peak spring flavor.

5. Make a well in the center of the bulgur, add a little more avocado oil, and break the eggs into the well. Gently fold the eggs into the bulgur and stir until set, 1 to 2 minutes.

6. Add the peas and stir to combine. Sprinkle with the lime juice, the remaining 1 tablespoon olive oil, the remaining 1 teaspoon salt, and a few cracks of pepper. Give everything a toss and allow it to cook for another 2 minutes for the flavors to come together. Stir in the chives and remove the pan from the heat.

7. Top with more chives and serve with garlicky tahini and harissa.

eggplant chickpea khoresh with buttery saffron rice

⅓ cup plus 2 tablespoons extra-virgin olive oil

1 large eggplant, peeled and cut into 1-inch pieces (see Note, page 265)

3½ teaspoons kosher salt

2 medium yellow onions, finely chopped

5 medium garlic cloves, finely chopped

1 teaspoon ground turmeric

Juicy pinch of saffron threads

Juicy pinch of ground cinnamon

¼ cup tomato paste

1 (15-ounce) can chickpeas, drained and rinsed (see Note, page 265)

1 (28-ounce) can crushed tomatoes (I like San Marzano)

½ cup finely chopped fresh cilantro leaves and stems

½ cup finely chopped fresh mint leaves, plus more for garnish

3 dried black limes, pierced a few times with a fork or sharp knife (see Note, page 147)

1 teaspoon fenugreek leaves (optional)

Juice of 1 lime

Buttery Saffron Rice (recipe follows), for serving

There's a large community of Persian Jews in Israel, and a signature dish that they brought with them is khoresh. The word *khoresh* just means "stew" or "stewed." With this recipe, I was inspired by a version of khoresh that makes eggplant the star (extremely valid), so I was going for a beautifully tangy and tart tomato-based broth that gets that bright tang from black limes but is also enriched with saffron, cinnamon, and fenugreek plus tender hunks of eggplant and chickpeas. Spooned over buttery saffron rice with a squeeze of fresh lime to really push it over the edge, it's the ultimate feel-good dish.

1. Heat ⅓ cup of the olive oil in a large skillet over medium-high heat. When the oil shimmers, add the eggplant and season with 1 teaspoon of the salt. Sauté, stirring occasionally, until lightly golden, about 10 minutes. Remove the pan from the heat and set aside.

2. Heat the remaining 2 tablespoons olive oil in a large pot over medium heat. Add the onions, garlic, 1½ teaspoons of the salt, the turmeric, saffron, and cinnamon and sauté, stirring occasionally, until the onions are lightly golden, about 5 minutes.

3. Add the tomato paste and cook, stirring, until it darkens in color, about 1 minute. Add the reserved eggplant and the chickpeas and toss to coat. Stir in the crushed tomatoes, then fill the can with water and add that to the pot too. Add the cilantro, mint, dried limes, and fenugreek (if using) and stir to combine.

4. Bring the pot to a simmer, cover, and reduce the heat to low. Allow the stew to simmer

recipe continues

grains on grains on pasta

Note: This would also be delicious with zucchini instead of the eggplant and kidney beans instead of chickpeas.

for 30 minutes. Remove the pot from the heat. I don't remove the limes; I just serve around them, but feel free to remove and discard.

5. Squeeze the lime juice over the top, adjust the seasoning with the remaining 1 teaspoon salt, if needed, and serve over the buttery rice.

buttery saffron rice

This is your new staple rice. It's like the perfect white tee. The saffron lends it the subtlest earthy-sweet flavor and golden color, while butter does what it does best. Mound all your veg and stews on top, transform it into Sunny Cherry Rice (page 255), or eat it on its own.

MAKES 3 CUPS

2 tablespoons salted butter

Pinch of saffron threads

1 cup basmati rice, rinsed until the water runs clear

½ teaspoon kosher salt

1. In a medium pot, combine the butter and saffron over medium heat. When the butter has melted, add the rice and salt and stir to coat well with the saffron butter.

2. Add 2 cups of water and bring to a boil over medium-high heat. Cover, reduce the heat to medium-low, and simmer until the liquid has been absorbed and the rice is tender, 10 to 12 minutes.

3. Turn off the heat and keep the pot covered for 10 minutes. When ready to serve, fluff the rice with a fork.

charred turmeric cauli with israeli couscous and chile mint vinaigrette

FOR THE TURMERIC CAULIFLOWER

6 tablespoons extra-virgin olive oil

2 teaspoons kosher salt

1 teaspoon ground turmeric

2 medium heads cauliflower, cut into 1- to 2-inch florets

FOR THE ISRAELI COUSCOUS AND CHILE MINT VINAIGRETTE

½ cup plus 1 tablespoon extra-virgin olive oil

1 cup Israeli (pearled) couscous (see Note)

Grated zest and juice of 1 lemon

2 tablespoons finely chopped fresh mint, plus small leaves for garnish

1 tablespoon honey

¾ teaspoon Aleppo pepper or red chile flakes

¾ teaspoon kosher salt

¼ cup currants or black raisins, soaked in warm water for 10 minutes and drained

¼ cup sliced almonds, toasted in a dry pan until fragrant

Note: You could substitute 2 cups cooked orzo for the couscous.

Israeli couscous, also known as ptitim or pearl couscous, is basically like a toasted pasta shaped into tiny balls—and it's the ultimate blank slate when it comes to soaking up flavor. But even though this is such a straightforward workhorse kind of a dish that comes together super quickly, it's high maintenance in *spirit*. The cauliflower gets all chewy and meaty when slathered with turmeric oil and roasted until caramelized, the couscous gets some interest and texture from raisins and almonds, and everything drinks up a minty, chile-laced vinaigrette. It's a dish that's regularly sitting in my fridge for last-minute lunches and midday munches, but it would also shine on a dinner table.

1. Preheat the oven to 500°F.

2. **Make the cauliflower:** In a large bowl, stir together the olive oil, salt, and turmeric. Add the cauliflower florets and toss to coat well, making sure to get into all the crannies.

3. Spread the cauliflower over a baking sheet in a single layer and roast for 25 to 35 minutes, tossing about halfway through, until the cauliflower is deeply caramelized and charred in places.

4. **While the cauliflower roasts, make the couscous:** Heat 1 tablespoon of the olive oil in a medium pot over medium heat. When the oil shimmers, add the couscous and toast until lightly brown, 1 to 2 minutes. Add 1¼ cups of water and allow the pot to come to a boil. Reduce to a simmer and cover. Cook over low heat until the water has been absorbed, about 15 minutes. Set aside.

5. Make the vinaigrette:
In a medium bowl, whisk together the lemon zest and juice, mint, honey, Aleppo, and salt. While whisking, slowly stream in the remaining ½ cup olive oil and whisk until fully incorporated.

6. Drizzle half of the vinaigrette over the couscous and toss to combine. Fold in the currants. Transfer the couscous to a serving bowl and top with the cauliflower. Finish with the remaining vinaigrette, the almonds, and some fresh mint.

pine nut and preserved lemon pasta

Serves 4 to 6

6 tablespoons (¾ stick) unsalted butter

3 medium garlic cloves, finely sliced

2½ tablespoons rinsed and chopped rind of Preserved Lemons (page 67)

1 teaspoon Aleppo pepper or red chile flakes, plus more for serving

3 tablespoons plus ½ teaspoon kosher salt

1 (16-ounce) package spaghetti

½ cup pine nuts, lightly toasted in a dry pan

1 cup freshly grated Parmesan, plus more for serving

Juice of ½ lemon

Freshly ground black pepper to taste

This is date night—'70s Spotify playlist on the speakers, a chilled bottle of white on the table, and a pot of this pasta on the stove. I owe a lot of this happiness to Missy Robbins, an amazing chef and friend, who introduced me to her brilliant and approachable pine nut pasta. With a very small handful of ingredients—mainly butter, garlic, Parm, and pasta—she showed me how fatty, nutty pine nuts can completely steal the show. I made my own version by adding a couple of my favorite staples, preserved lemons and Aleppo pepper, into the mix, and the tart heat makes it straight-up addicting. I'm not saying it's foreplay on a plate, but I'm not saying it's not.

1. In a large skillet over medium heat, combine the butter, garlic, and preserved lemon. When the butter has melted, add the Aleppo and ½ teaspoon of the salt and remove from the heat.

2. Bring a large pot of water to a boil over medium-high heat and season with the remaining 3 tablespoons salt. Add the pasta and cook according to the package instructions for al dente. Reserve 1½ cups of the cooking water and set aside.

3. Add the pasta directly to the butter sauce along with all but 2 tablespoons of the pine nuts. Top with ½ cup of the Parm, the lemon juice, and 1 cup of the reserved cooking water. Mix with a wooden spoon until the sauce starts to emulsify and coat the pasta. Add the remaining ½ cup cheese and, if needed, more cooking water to help loosen the sauce.

4. Serve topped with the reserved pine nuts, a bit more Parm, and a sprinkle of Aleppo and black pepper.

spiced harissa orecchiette with garlicky tahini

—————————————————————————————————— Serves 4 to 6

FOR THE PASTA

3 tablespoons kosher salt

1 (16-ounce) package orecchiette

FOR THE SPICED HARISSA TOMATO SAUCE

⅓ cup extra-virgin olive oil

2 large shallots, finely chopped

¾ teaspoon kosher salt

Freshly ground black pepper to taste

3 garlic cloves, thinly sliced

1½ teaspoons fennel seeds, crushed with a mortar in a pestle

¼ teaspoon ground coriander

⅓ cup Fast 'n' Fresh Harissa (page 33)

3 cups cherry tomatoes

Handful of fresh basil leaves, plus small leaves for garnish

FOR SERVING

Garlicky Tahini (page 59)

Grated zest from 1 lemon

I went back and forth on whether this cookbook, especially a book devoted to Middle Eastern–inspired cooking, needed a red-sauce pasta dish. But then I considered that when it comes to quick, satisfying meals, pasta is going to be your girl every single time. But I also had to make it my own, so I took a classic fennel-y cherry tomato sauce to the shuk and dolled her up with spicy harissa and ribbons of garlicky tahini. I dare you not to make this once a week.

1. **Start the pasta:** Fill a large pot with water, add the salt, and bring to a boil over medium-high heat.

2. **While the water comes to a boil, make the sauce:** Heat the oil in a large skillet with a fitted lid over medium heat. When the oil shimmers, reduce the heat to medium-low, add the shallots, and season with the salt and a couple cracks of pepper. Sauté, stirring occasionally, until the shallots are translucent and lightly golden, 8 to 10 minutes. Add the garlic, fennel, and coriander and cook just until the garlic begins to turn lightly golden and the spices are fragrant, about 1 minute.

3. Stir in the harissa and cook until it deepens in color, about 2 minutes. It may separate, but it will come back together as the tomatoes cook. Add the tomatoes and ¼ cup of water, stir to combine, and cover the pan. Reduce the heat to medium-low and cook, stirring occasionally, until the tomatoes are broken down and saucy, about 20 minutes. You can use the back of your spoon to encourage them to melt.

4. **While the tomatoes cook down, finish the pasta:** Add the orecchiette to the boiling water and cook according to the package instructions for al dente. Once it is al dente, reserve 1 cup of the pasta water and then drain.

5. **While the pasta cooks, finish the dish:** Remove the lid from the sauce and allow it to simmer until it is thick enough to cling to the pasta, about 10 more minutes. Stir in the basil and keep the pan over the lowest heat setting as you wait for the pasta to finish cooking.

6. Add the cooked pasta directly to the sauce and toss to combine. Add pasta cooking water ¼ cup at a time until the sauce reaches the consistency you like.

7. Transfer the pasta to a serving bowl and finish with a drizzle of garlicky tahini and the lemon zest. Garnish with basil, serve with spoons, and shovel into your mouth.

CHAPTER 9

sweetness

I will say it if no one else does: The baked goods in Israel are supreme. Everywhere you go, there are bakeries cranking out **buttery**, **creamy**, **flaky**, **lusciously moist** (sorry, not sorry) **yeasted/fruit-stuffed/herb-infused/chocolate-coated** deliciousness. And it tracks—Israelis take their sweets very seriously and do not confine them to just after dinner. In fact, it's even more common that people are making and buying cakes, cookies, and loaves to keep on their counter in the event of a friend stopping over or, more likely, to enjoy with their obligatory afternoon coffee. If there's one thing we can all take away from this chapter, it's that we need to be leaning more into **coffee and treat time**, but also, these recipes will serve you no matter the occasion or craving.

pull-apart tahini rugelach

Makes 40 rugelach

FOR THE DOUGH

¾ cup whole milk

½ cup granulated sugar, plus a pinch

2¼ teaspoons (1 packet) active dry yeast

4½ cups all-purpose flour, plus more for dusting

3 large eggs plus 1 large egg yolk

1 teaspoon vanilla extract

Grated zest of 1 lemon

1 teaspoon kosher salt

8 tablespoons (1 stick) unsalted butter, room temperature, plus more for greasing

FOR THE TAHINI FILLING

1 cup tahini (see Note, page 279)

1 cup confectioners' sugar

1 teaspoon vanilla extract

1 teaspoon kosher salt

FOR THE SESAME SIMPLE SYRUP

¼ cup sesame seeds

½ cup granulated sugar

When Ido and I remodeled our current house, which was our first official house-house, it was mainly with the intention of having a cozy crash pad for anyone who would ever want to come over and hang out. And of course, if you're going to come to my house, then I'm going to stuff you full of food. Which is why I love having a roster of dishes that I know will not only feed a crowd but totally wow them. Just the smell of these baking will make you feel like the Most-est Hostess, but once you set down the pan and let everyone pull apart these gooey, pillowy Israeli-style rugelach—which are essentially yeasted brioche buns stuffed with a sweet tahini filling—you'll officially become *that* girl. And everyone wants to be that girl.

1. **Make the dough:** In a small saucepan over medium-low heat, warm the milk with a pinch of sugar until the milk is almost hot, or just about body temperature, 1 to 2 minutes. (Take care not to let the milk get too hot or it will kill the yeast!) Add the yeast and let it bloom for about 5 minutes, until foamy.

2. Transfer the mixture to a stand mixer fitted with the dough hook. Add the flour, sugar, whole eggs, vanilla, and lemon zest and mix on medium speed until just combined, about 2 minutes. Sprinkle in the salt and mix until the dough has formed a ball, about 1 minute.

3. Add the butter 1 tablespoon at a time, mixing well between additions, until it is completely incorporated. Continue mixing for 10 to 15 minutes, pausing occasionally to scrape down the sides of the bowl with a spatula, until the dough is smooth and no longer sticking to the bowl. Transfer to another medium bowl lightly greased with butter. Cover the bowl with a damp towel and

recipe continues

allow the dough to rise in a warm place until doubled in size, 1 to 1½ hours.

4. **While the dough proofs, make the filling:** In a stand mixer fitted with the paddle attachment, combine the tahini, confectioners' sugar, vanilla, and salt. Mix on medium speed until well combined and smooth, about 2 minutes.

5. **Assemble the rugelach:** Line a baking sheet with parchment paper or a silicone baking mat.

6. Turn out the dough onto a lightly floured work surface and divide it into four even pieces. Keep three pieces covered with a towel in the fridge while you work with the first piece. Use a rolling pin to roll the dough into a rectangle as thin as you can make it without tearing the dough (see Note). Use a spatula to spread a quarter of the filling mixture evenly over the dough. Fold the dough in half widthwise (bringing the two short ends of the rectangle to meet) and use a rolling pin to roll the dough as thin as you can reasonably make it.

7. Use a sharp knife to cut the dough into thin triangles, about 1 inch wide at the base. (You should get about ten.) Beginning with the base of each triangle, roll up the dough, gently pressing as you go to help flatten it, to the tip. Transfer the finished rugelach to the prepared baking sheet, keeping them evenly spaced, and continue with the remaining pieces of dough and filling. (It's okay for them to not have a lot of space, because they'll fuse to create that break-apart feel we're going for.) Repeat with the remaining portions of dough and filling. Cover the dough with a towel and set aside to proof until puffed, about 1 hour.

8. Preheat the oven to 350°F.

9. In a small bowl, use a fork to beat together the egg yolk with 1 tablespoon of water. Brush the egg wash over the rugelach and bake for 25 to 30 minutes, until golden.

10. **While the rugelach bake, make the syrup:** In a small pot over medium heat, toast the sesame seeds until lightly golden, about 2 minutes.

Note: The trick here is to roll out the dough as thin as you can, which will ensure you get as many layers as possible in your rugelach. Also, you could change up the flavor and use 1½ cups of Nutella in place of the tahini filling.

Transfer the sesame seeds to a small bowl and set aside. To the same pot, add the granulated sugar and ½ cup of water and bring to a boil over medium-high heat. Reduce to a simmer and heat until the sugar has dissolved, about 1 minute. Add the sesame seeds back in and pour the syrup over the hot rugelach when they come out of the oven.

11. To serve, I like bringing the entire tray out to the table and letting people have at it.

12. Wrap leftovers in plastic wrap and store in a sealed container at room temperature for up to 1 week. Reheat in the microwave for max fluffiness, about 20 seconds on high heat, or warm in the oven at 325°F for 5 to 7 minutes.

sage-honey semifreddo

Serves 8 to 10

2 cups heavy cream

10 fresh sage leaves

½ cup full-fat Greek yogurt

⅓ cup honey, plus more
for serving

1 teaspoon vanilla extract

¼ teaspoon kosher salt

2 large eggs plus 2 large
egg yolks

¼ cup sugar

1 cup crushed raw walnuts,
toasted in a dry pan until
fragrant

Extra-virgin olive oil, for serving

Flaky sea salt, for serving

The sage steeped into this creamy frozen mousse made with honey and drizzled with olive oil is honestly the next best thing to a trip to the Mediterranean. Plus, it's the perfect not-too-heavy sweet treat to end a meal. Freezing the semifreddo does take a minute, but the prep time is minimal, and you can make this ahead. Then, when you whip it out and no one is expecting it? Boom. That's some domestic goddess shit right there.

1. Line a 9 × 5-inch loaf pan with plastic wrap, leaving a 3- to 4-inch overhang on each side.

2. In a small pot, bring the cream to a simmer over medium-low heat. Add the sage and turn off the heat. Let the cream cool completely, then transfer it to the fridge to chill for at least 1 hour or up to overnight.

3. Discard the sage, giving it a good squeeze first so you wring out all that flavor. Transfer the cream to a large bowl and, using a hand mixer on medium-high speed or a whisk, whip the cream until soft peaks form. Whisk in the yogurt, honey, vanilla, and salt until just combined. Set aside.

4. Bring a small pot of water to a boil and reduce to a simmer. In a medium heatproof bowl, combine the whole eggs, egg yolks, and sugar. Set the bowl over the simmering water and whisk vigorously until the mixture gets light, airy, and glossy, 8 to 10 minutes. (You can do it!) You'll know it's done when you lift the whisk out of the mixture and you get a nice ribbon that sits on the surface for a moment before reincorporating.

5. While gently mixing with a spatula, add about ½ cup of the egg mixture to the whipped cream until combined. Add the remaining egg mixture and fold until evenly combined.

recipe continues

sweetness

281

6. Sprinkle the walnuts in the bottom of the prepared pan and pour the mixture over the top. Fold up the extra plastic wrap to cover, then chill in the freezer for at least 6 hours but preferably overnight.

7. To serve, flip the semifreddo onto a plate and finish with a drizzle of olive oil and honey plus a sprinkle of flaky salt.

8. Store leftovers in a freezer-safe container in the freezer for up to 1 month.

mom's baked cheesecake

FOR THE CRUST

1⅓ cups all-purpose flour

½ teaspoon baking powder

⅓ cup sugar

8 tablespoons (1 stick) unsalted butter, room temperature

1 large egg

FOR THE FILLING

1 (8-ounce) package plain cream cheese, room temperature

1 (15-ounce) container pressed whole-milk ricotta or regular ricotta, strained in a cheesecloth or fine-mesh sieve

⅔ cup sugar, plus a pinch

6 large eggs, separated

1 tablespoon cornstarch

1 teaspoon vanilla extract

My mom got the recipe for this cake from a friend when my sisters and I were little, and she's been treating us to it ever since—including bringing me an entire cake of my own whenever she'd visit me at overnight camp. (Which I'd keep next to my bunk and eat by myself without any shame; sorry 'bout ya 'cause it's my camp cake.) It's the kind of light, airy cheesecake that, despite its buttery shell of a crust, is neither too sweet nor too rich, so you can make it early in the day and have it for breakfast, or graze on it all day by the handful while you stand in front of the fridge. Just thinking about how much this cake has been a part of my life makes me so happy, especially when my daughters light up every time they get to enjoy it, especially at Bubbie's house.

1. Make the crust: In a medium bowl, whisk together the flour and baking powder.

2. In a stand mixer fitted with the paddle attachment, combine the sugar and butter and beat on medium speed until fluffy and light, about 3 minutes. Add the egg and mix until fully incorporated. Add the flour mixture and mix on medium-low speed until just incorporated.

3. Press the dough into the bottom and completely up the sides of a 9-inch springform pan. Chill the crust in the fridge while you make the filling.

4. Preheat the oven to 325°F.

5. Make the filling: In a food processor, combine the cream cheese, ricotta, and sugar and process until very creamy and well combined. Pause and scrape down the sides of the bowl with a spatula as needed.

recipe continues

6. Add the egg yolks one at a time, making sure each is well incorporated before adding the next. Add the cornstarch and vanilla and process until thoroughly mixed. Transfer the mixture to a large bowl and set aside.

7. In a stand mixer fitted with the whisk attachment, whip the egg whites and a pinch of sugar on medium-high speed until they form stiff peaks, 5 minutes. (You could also do this in a large bowl with a whisk if you like a challenge.)

8. Pour a third of the egg whites into the cream cheese mixture and gently fold it in. Repeat with the remaining egg whites, working in thirds and taking care not to lose any of that air!

9. Pour the filling into the crust. Slightly lift and drop the pan onto the counter a couple times to release any large air bubbles.

10. Bake for 1 hour and 10 minutes to 1 hour and 20 minutes until the top of the cheesecake is lightly golden and puffed and the center is set but the top wobbles a bit (like a soufflé). The top will crack, but that's okay; it's part of the look.

11. Allow the cake to cool completely before serving. Let it chill in the fridge for at least 1 hour.

12. Slice and serve or snack. Store covered in the fridge for up to 1 week (but it won't last that long, I promise).

strawberry rhubarb rose tahini crumble

Makes one 8 × 10-inch crumble (serves 8)

FOR THE STRAWBERRY RHUBARB ROSE FILLING

1¼ pounds fresh rhubarb, sliced into ½-inch pieces

1¼ pounds fresh strawberries, hulled and sliced

⅔ cup granulated sugar

3 tablespoons cornstarch

Juice of 1 lemon

1½ teaspoons rose water or orange blossom water (optional; see Notes)

½ teaspoon vanilla extract

¼ teaspoon kosher salt

FOR THE TAHINI CRUMBLE TOPPING

⅔ cup all-purpose flour

½ cup sesame seeds, toasted in a dry pan until fragrant

6 tablespoons light brown sugar

¼ cup rolled oats

½ teaspoon kosher salt

4 tablespoons (½ stick) unsalted butter, melted

¼ cup tahini

FOR SERVING

Vanilla ice cream or Labaneh (page 42)

My biggest reason for including a crumble in this book is that I want to remind everyone that it's the perfect dessert. It requires very little beyond stirring together a handful of ingredients (which you could do in advance); you can use any fruit you have on hand (preferably seasonal, especially if you are like me and have no self-control at the market and buy more than you can eat every single time); and after it's done its thing in the oven, you have this bubbling, jammy dream. For this version, we're using the classic spring/summer combo of strawberries and rhubarb and taming any tartness with the subtlest hint of rose. (I promise we're not going for potpourri here.) And because we're adding tahini to the topping, you get this crispy, buttery, cookie-like crumble that you could actually just bake off as cookies instead. If that is not perfection, I really don't know what is.

1. Make the filling: In a large bowl, combine the rhubarb, strawberries, granulated sugar, cornstarch, lemon juice, rose water (if using), vanilla, and salt. Stir well to coat the fruit and set aside to macerate while you make the crumble topping.

2. Set a rack in the middle of the oven and preheat the oven to 375°F. Line a baking sheet with parchment paper.

3. Make the topping: In a medium bowl, stir together the flour, sesame seeds, brown sugar, oats, and salt. Add the melted butter and tahini and stir until clumps form.

4. Transfer the fruit and all the juices into an 8 × 10-inch baking dish (see Notes) and set it on top of the prepared baking sheet. Crumble the topping over the fruit in large chunks. Bake for 50 to 60 minutes, until the topping is golden brown and the fruit is bubbling.

If the topping begins to burn before the crumble is ready, cover the baking dish with foil.

5. To serve: Allow the crumble to cool for 1 hour before serving with ice cream or dollops of labaneh. Store leftovers in a sealed container in the fridge for 3 to 5 days; reheat in the oven at 350°F for a few minutes before eating.

Notes: Rose or orange blossom water does add something special here, but if you don't have any handy, don't let that stand in the way of making this crumble.

You could also bake this in a 9-inch square or round baking dish.

tahini fudge pops

FOR THE FUDGE POPS

1 (14-ounce) can full-fat coconut milk

½ cup tahini

½ cup maple syrup

½ cup unsweetened oat milk

⅓ cup Dutch-process cocoa powder

½ teaspoon kosher salt

FOR THE CHOCOLATE SHELL TOPPING

8 ounces dark chocolate (72% cacao), chopped

1 tablespoon coconut oil

FOR ASSEMBLY

½ cup crumbled halva or crushed Honey-Sesame Candied Matzo (see Note, page 294)

Flaky sea salt

I feel like Fudgsicles were the dessert staple of the '80s and '90s. They certainly were in the Grinshpan household, and they still have a chokehold on me. I mean, is it ice cream? Is it an ice pop? Is it guaranteed brain freeze because no matter how hard you tried to resist you had to get all up in there with your teeth? This version is just as rich and substantial, thanks largely to the addition of tahini.

1. **Make the fudge pops:** In a blender, combine the coconut milk, tahini, maple syrup, oat milk, cocoa powder, and salt. Blend until smooth.

2. Divide the mixture among eight wells of a 2-ounce ice pop mold. (They should be filled to the top.) Freeze until the tops of the pops are semifirm, 10 to 20 minutes. Insert a wooden ice pop stick into each and freeze until firm, at least 2 hours or up to several days.

3. **Just before serving, make the chocolate shell:** Combine the chocolate and coconut oil in a medium microwave-safe bowl and microwave on high in 30-second intervals, stirring between each, until completely melted, about 2 minutes total.

4. **Assemble:** Transfer the chocolate mixture to a cup wide enough to fit a pop.

5. Line a large plate or baking sheet with parchment paper. Briefly run the bottom of the ice pop molds under warm water (this will help release the fudge pops). Pull out each pop, dunk the top two-thirds in the melted chocolate, and immediately sprinkle with the halva or sesame candy and the flaky salt. Place on the prepared plate or baking sheet and transfer to the freezer to set, about 15 minutes.

6. Store the pops in a sealed container in the freezer for up to 1 month. Let them sit at room temperature for 2 to 3 minutes before eating for an ultrafudgy texture.

portokalopita

FOR THE HONEY ORANGE SYRUP

1½ cups fresh orange juice

¾ cup granulated sugar

¼ cup honey

FOR THE CAKE

½ cup extra-virgin olive oil, plus more for greasing

8 ounces phyllo dough sheets, thawed

½ cup packed light brown sugar

2 large eggs

¾ cup full-fat Greek yogurt, plus more for serving

1½ teaspoons baking powder

Grated zest of 1 orange

¼ teaspoon kosher salt

½ teaspoon ground cinnamon

Note: Instead of drying out the phyllo in the oven, you could leave it out overnight.

In Tel Aviv, there is an adorable café called Mirage owned by Eyal Shani (I clearly have a thing for his food). One time they had this incredibly moist, dense-looking cake with tons of flaky layers, and when I asked the barista what it was, he just said "portokalopita" (porto-kah-LOW-pita)—as if everyone had heard of it. I looked it up when I left, and saw that it's a Greek cake made from dried-out phyllo that's been soaked in custard. It's sun-kissed and citrusy, and it's also traditionally made using scraps of phyllo, which is a great hack if you're already making another phyllo recipe in this book.

1. Make the syrup: In a medium saucepan, stir together the orange juice, granulated sugar, and honey. Bring the mixture to a boil over medium-high heat, then reduce the heat to medium. Allow the mixture to simmer, stirring occasionally, until it reduces by half, 15 to 20 minutes. Set aside to cool.

2. While the syrup simmers, start the cake: Preheat the oven to 200°F. Lightly coat a 9 × 5-inch loaf pan with olive oil and line with parchment paper. Line a baking sheet with parchment paper.

3. Spread the phyllo sheets over the prepared baking sheet, pulling apart some of the layers.

It's okay if they get rumpled! Bake for 20 to 25 minutes, until dry and flaky (see Note). Set aside and increase the oven temperature to 350°F.

4. In the bowl of a stand mixer fitted with the paddle attachment, combine the brown sugar and eggs. Beat on high speed until fluffy, 3 to 4 minutes. Add the yogurt, olive oil, baking powder, orange zest, salt, and cinnamon and mix until just combined.

5. Gradually add the phyllo to the batter in three additions, mixing on low speed until all the phyllo is incorporated. Pour the mixture into the prepared pan and bake for 45 to 55 minutes,

tahini baby

until the top is golden brown and a knife inserted into the center comes out clean.

6. Ladle the syrup over the hot cake, letting each ladle of syrup absorb before adding the next. Repeat until three-quarters of the syrup has been used.

7. Slice and serve with a dollop of Greek yogurt and drizzle with the remaining syrup. Store leftovers in a sealed container at room temperature for up to 1 week

honey-sesame candied matzo

Serves 8 to 12

1 teaspoon extra-virgin olive oil, plus more for greasing

2½ matzo squares (see Note, page 294)

½ cup honey

½ cup packed dark brown sugar

1 teaspoon kosher salt

2 tablespoons unsalted butter

2 cups sesame seeds, plus more for garnish, toasted in a dry pan until golden and fragrant

6 ounces bittersweet chocolate, chopped

Flaky sea salt and/or shredded halva, for garnish

If you grew up somewhere predominantly Jewish, like my child-hood neighborhood in Toronto, there's a good chance that you've seen a bowlful of those individually wrapped sesame-coated tof-fee candies at the checkout counter at Jewish delis or at a bubbie's house. I've always loved the syrupy floral sweetness of the honey combined with an absurd amount of nutty sesame, which I wanted to combine with another favorite dessert among members of the tribe: matzo coated in toffee and chocolate. I added that sesame overload to the toffee and ended up with a confection that blends the best of both worlds in one stupidly simple, deeply obsession-worthy sweet-salty treat.

1. Lightly coat a spatula with olive oil and set aside. Line a baking sheet with parchment paper and arrange the matzo on top so that the pieces are touching. Set aside.

2. In a medium pot, combine the honey, brown sugar, and salt. Bring the mixture to a boil over medium heat, stirring constantly. Boil for 2 minutes, until the mixture darkens slightly.

3. Stir in the butter. When it has melted completely, add the sesame seeds and olive oil and let the mixture come to

a boil, continuing to stir. Heat for another 2 minutes, until the mixture is nice and thick.

4. Immediately pour the candied sesame mixture over the matzo. Use your oiled spatula to spread the mixture into a smooth, even layer that completely covers the matzo. Transfer the baking sheet to the freezer and chill until the matzo is hardened, about 15 minutes.

5. Meanwhile, place the chocolate in a microwave-

recipe continues

Note: You can skip the matzo and make this as a toffee-like candy instead. Just pour the caramel into a greased, parchment paper–lined 9-inch pan and let it set. Cut into rectangles and enjoy, or crumble it up and use it as a topping for Tahini Fudge Pops (page 289).

safe bowl and microwave in 30-second intervals, stirring between each, until melted, about 2 minutes total. Pour the chocolate over the set candied matzo, using a spatula to spread it in a smooth, even layer that completely covers the matzo.

6. Immediately sprinkle with flaky salt, toasted sesame seeds, and/or shredded halva. Transfer the baking sheet back to the freezer until the chocolate is set, about 15 minutes. Break up the candied matzo into big, delicious pieces and serve.

7. The candied matzo can be stored in an airtight container at room temperature for up to 7 days or in the freezer for up to 2 weeks.

salty vanilla bean krembo tart

FOR THE CRUST

8 tablespoons (1 stick) salted butter, melted, plus more for greasing

18 graham cracker "sheets"

FOR THE FILLING

1 (8-ounce) package plain cream cheese, room temperature

1½ cups (about 7 ounces) marshmallow crème (see Notes, page 296)

1½ tablespoons confectioners' sugar

2 teaspoons vanilla extract or vanilla bean paste (see Notes, page 296)

Pinch of kosher salt

1½ cups heavy cream

FOR THE TOPPING

¾ cup (6 ounces) chopped bittersweet chocolate

1½ tablespoons extra-virgin olive oil

Flaky sea salt, for serving

Ido's favorite sweets growing up were krembos, marshmallow cream puffs with a butter cookie base and thin chocolate shell. And to make them even more special, they were only sold between fall and winter, when they wouldn't instantly melt in the desert heat. I distinctly remember walking through Tel Aviv with Ido on one of our first trips to Israel together, when he saw a krembo and lost his damn mind. Even though I already knew what they were, I let him mansplain it to me all over again because he was so clearly passionate about it. (And I loved him.) In his honor, I've made a full-size tart version of this treat, complete with buttery cookie crust, fluffy marshmallow center (which we're using fluff for because we don't fuck around with making marshmallows from scratch in this house), and Magic Shell–like chocolate coating. It's sweet-on-sweet-on-sweet in the best possible way, and a taste of childhood at its finest.

I love to keep this dessert in the freezer and serve it VERY cold on a hot day. Freezing also makes it easy to slice very thin and nibble on as the perfect after-dinner bite.

1. **Make the crust:** Preheat the oven to 350°F. Lightly grease an 11-inch tart pan with butter.

2. In a food processor, process the graham crackers until they're finely ground and powdery; you should have about 2 cups of crumbs. Add the melted butter and process again until the mixture looks and feels like wet sand.

3. Use your hands to firmly press the mixture into the bottom and sides of the pan. You want to use the bottom of a glass to get a nice, thin, even crust. Chill in the fridge for 10 minutes before baking. (This will help make the crust nice and sturdy.)

recipe continues

Notes: Instead of marshmallow fluff, you could add 14 ounces of marshmallows to a stand mixer fitted with the paddle attachment and beat on high until the mixture is smooth. Then continue with the recipe as written.

For extra vanilla bean flavor, you could use vanilla bean paste here, which you can find in the baking aisle of most grocery stores or online. But vanilla extract will also get the job done.

4. Bake the crust for 10 to 12 minutes, until golden around the edges. Allow the crust to cool completely on a cooling rack, about 30 minutes.

5. While the crust cools, make the filling: In a blender or food processor, combine the cream cheese, marshmallow crème, confectioners' sugar, vanilla, and salt and blend or process until completely smooth. Set aside.

6. In a stand mixer fitted with the paddle attachment, whip the cream on medium-high speed until it holds medium-stiff peaks, about 6 minutes. Use a spatula to gently fold in the marshmallow mixture, then spread the marshmallow cream evenly and smoothly over the cooled crust. Freeze

for at least 2 hours or up to 4 days to set.

7. When ready to assemble, make the topping: In a small microwave-safe bowl, combine the chocolate and olive oil. Microwave in 30-second intervals, stirring between them, until fully melted, about 2 minutes total.

8. Slowly pour the chocolate over the chilled tart, rotating the tart as you pour to ensure a smooth, even coating. Sprinkle with flaky salt and chill to firm up the topping, about 15 minutes.

9. Slice and serve. Freeze the leftovers (wrapped in plastic or foil) and shave off pieces when you're in the mood for an ice cream tart–like treat.

all-day fennel and sesame shortbread cookies

Makes 12 cookies

⅔ cup granulated sugar

1 teaspoon fennel seeds

1½ cups all-purpose flour

1 teaspoon kosher salt

10 tablespoons unsalted butter

¼ cup tahini

1 large egg

2 tablespoons demerara sugar

2 tablespoons sesame seeds

Thought I'd leave my obsession with fennel for the savory dishes? Guess again! I love the sweet licorice-ness of fennel seeds in baked goods. Fennel and sesame is a classic Levantine dessert pairing, plus fennel is a traditional flavor to enjoy after dinner because it's so clean and fresh. (Fennel seeds have natural digestion-boosting properties, but let's be honest, we're putting them in a butter cookie.) These scratch the itch for something sweet but still feel light and balanced--like a slice and bake cookie on a whole other level.

1. In a high-speed blender, combine the granulated sugar and fennel and blend until fragrant and well incorporated, about 10 seconds.

2. In a medium bowl, whisk together the fennel sugar, flour, and salt. Set aside.

3. Melt the butter in a small pan over medium heat, swirling occasionally. Remove from the heat and let cool slightly, about 5 minutes.

4. Whisk in the tahini, then transfer the mixture to the bowl with the dry ingredients. Stir to combine, then use your hands to press the dough into a ball as best you can (it may be a little crumbly, and that's okay!).

5. Turn out the dough onto a 12-inch piece of plastic wrap. Add a second sheet of plastic wrap on top, then gently roll the dough into a roughly 1½-inch-thick log. Enclose the dough in plastic and refrigerate until firm, about 2 hours.

6. Preheat the oven to 350°F. Line a baking sheet with parchment paper.

7. In a small bowl, use a fork to beat the egg. On a large plate, stir together the demerara sugar and sesame seeds.

8. Brush the outside of the dough with the egg, then roll it in the sesame sugar. Slice the log into ¾-inch-thick rounds and arrange them on the

prepared baking sheet, sliced
side down, about 1 inch apart.

9. Bake for 15 to 20 minutes,
until the edges are just
beginning to brown.

Store the cookies in a
sealed container at room
temperature for up to 1 week.

Writing a book is an incredibly long and involved process, and it truly takes a village to bring it to life. I love this village, and I feel beyond fortunate that I get to work with such unbelievably talented people, who took this idea and made it my literal dream book. Everyone mentioned here made this book what it is. The love, creativity, vision . . . it wouldn't be what it is without these people, whom I now feel so lucky to call my friends. I'm also excited to give a shout-out to my loving and supportive family. None of this would have been possible without you.

Starting with my incredible agent, Eve Attermann. Eve, I can't tell you what it means to not only have you as my agent but also get to call you my friend. Your belief in me has carried me through these game-/life-changing projects. Thank you for your support, guidance, and enthusiasm for this book. It's exactly how we got here, and I can't thank you enough.

My editor, Lucia Watson—my ray of sunshine! Always so positive, your energy and enthusiasm kept me going. I absolutely LOVED working with you on our *Tahini Baby*, and the collaborative aspect was truly one of my favorite parts. You have always supported my ideas and then taken them to a place I couldn't have dreamed of. I love our book baby and feel so lucky that you said yes to making her come true.

Rachel Holtzman, my collaborator, it's official: You are family now. The hours we have spent kibbitzing, laughing, commiserating, and just chatting about all things food and family over the last couple years have really impacted me in more ways than you will ever know. Your ability to explain and express everything—all the stories, recipes, inspirations—has made this project what it is: a dream book. *My* dream book. The amount of hard work and dedication you put into your craft shows. You truly are the best at what you do, and I feel so grateful and lucky that we get to do this together.

Ashley Tucker, thank you for designing the most beautiful book. Your patience with me has not gone unnoticed. And it's led to the perfect, gorgeous outcome that is the exact vision we all had.

To the Avery team: Tracy Behar, Lindsay Gordon, Casey Maloney, Farin Schlussel, and Alyssa Adler, I'm so beyond lucky that we get to do this together. Each and every one of you has been a dream to work with, and I truly hope we get to do it again soon.

My photographer, Chris Bernabeo—you're the best! So talented, so sweet, and so open-minded. I loved every second with you on set.

Your ability to be so humble yet so talented just blows my mind. These pictures and the vibe are exactly what we envisioned. I will forever cherish these pictures and our time together listening to Taylor Swift for HOURS while watching you collab with the rest of the crew on set. It truly gave me a high watching you all do your thing. Thank you for being so collaborative, open to bouncing ideas around, and hard-working, and for capturing the most beautiful pics.

Christopher St. Onge—you fucking legend. Seriously, your talent is crazy. You aren't just a food stylist; you are a creative director. Watching you bring these dishes to life and collaborate with everyone on set was one of the best parts of the shoot. These pictures are amazing, and your energy and enthusiasm give me life. It's because of YOU we were able to shoot every recipe and push through the sweaty (OMG so sweaty) and insane hours. You made this happen. Thank you for everything.

Jacquie Matthews and Allegra D'Agostini, you are both so fun, hardworking, and great to be around. Thank you for hustling and making those incredibly long shoot days happen and with smiles on your faces. You are both so talented, and I can't wait to see where your culinary journey takes you next!

Prop stylist Jess Anderson, you have the most beautiful taste. I really couldn't even understand what you planned and prepped until it all came alive on our first shoot day—and then just kept getting better and better. Your props, colors, and patterns were beyond; you

truly brought this vision to life. Thank you! And Ross Anderson! You are such a sweet joy to be around. Thank you for all your hard work and for making my girls feel so special.

Chaya Rappoport, we truly have the same culinary vision and aesthetic, and I absolutely LOVED working with you. Having your hand in developing a selection of recipes for the book was such a fun and creative experience. I love your style and hope we get to cook together soon in the city!

Marissa Caputo, Sydnie Weiss, and the AIRE team—this book has been a long time coming for us. Thank you for your guidance, ideas, collaboration, friendship, and motivation. You gave me the confidence to bring my brand to the next level and then bring this book along with it. All the planning, prep, brainstorming, and lead-up were worth it! Here we are! *Tahini Baby* is here.

Mom and Dad—it's hard to put into words how grateful I am for you both and how lucky I am. You have been my biggest supporters from the beginning, pushing me to travel, to take chances—it's how I became the person I am to this day. I am a yes person because of you. Thank you for showing me the world and for teaching me everything I know. I love you. OH! And thank you for the backyard shoot day at your gorgeous house. It looks so goooood in the book! Also, thank you for letting me steal your cheesecake recipe for this book (even though I know you always said it was your friend's, but I feel like after making it for thirty-five years you can confidently just

call it your own) to share with everyone who will now bake it for their family and friends. I'm confident it will make them as happy as it made/makes all of us. To this day, still one of my favorite bites.

And finally, to my funny, fun, and always supportive lover of a sexy husband, Ido. You are always so game and so encouraging. You care with all your heart and put all of yourself into your family, your work, your home, your passions. I love how much you care and work so hard, always with a smile on your face and a pep in your step. Thank you for always holding my hand and for encouraging me to keep going but also at the same time encouraging me to pace myself and find the right balance. You always show up, and I can't thank you enough for it. Thank you for trying every dish in this book and for giving me the Ido confident thumbs-up. Your palate and your ideas are on fire, and I am so happy that everyone will now know that, since the recipes are 100 percent Ido-approved. AND you are a meat eater and never once said you missed meat during this entire process, which makes me even more thrilled that this book will land with so many cooks who want to lead a similar lifestyle to ours or are looking to try it.

Love our life and love you, more than you will ever know.

And to my girls, Ayv and Romi. Being your mom is the greatest joy and achievement in my life; nothing makes me prouder than watching you both become the people you are and are going to be. Thank you for your smiles, belly laughs, and boundless love.

Note: Bold page numbers indicate chapter subjects. Italicized page numbers indicate material in photographs.

index